岸本斉史

... of my friends are getting ...ed lately. It's too bad I'm ... busy to attend their weddings... I do so enjoy receptions.

—Masashi Kishimoto, 2007

Author/artist Masashi Kishimoto was born in 1974 in rural Okayama Prefecture, Japan. After spending time in art college, he won the Hop Step Award for new manga artists with his manga **Karakuri** (Mechanism). Kishimoto decided to base his next story on traditional Japanese culture. His first version of **Naruto**, drawn in 1997, was a one-shot story about fox spirits; his final version, which debuted in **Weekly Shonen Jump** in 1999, quickly became the most popular ninja manga in Japan.

NARUTO VOL. 38
SHONEN JUMP Manga Edition

STORY AND ART BY MASASHI KISHIMOTO

Translation/Mari Morimoto
English Adaptation/Naomi Kokubo, Eric-Jon Rössel Waugh
Touch-up Art & Lettering/Sabrina Heep
Design/Sean Lee
Editor/Joel Enos

Printed in the U.S.A.

Published by VIZ Media, LLC
P.O. Box 77010
San Francisco, CA 94107

10 9 8 7 6 5 4 3
First printing, March 2009
Third printing, December 2015

www.viz.com

PARENTAL ADVISORY
NARUTO is rated T for Teen and is recommended for ages 13 and up. This volume contains realistic and fantasy violence.

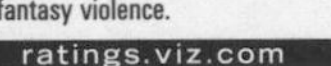

SHONEN JUMP MANGA EDITION

NARUTO

VOL. 38
PRACTICE MAKES PERFECT

STORY AND ART BY
MASASHI KISHIMOTO

Sakura
サクラ
Naruto
ナルト
Sasuke
サスケ
Sai
サイ
Yamato
ヤマト
Kakashi
カカシ

The Story So Far…

Naruto was once the bane of the Konohagakure Ninja Academy. Nevertheless, alongside his friends Sasuke and Sakura, he successfully joins the ranks of the ninja.

During the Chûnin Journeyman Ninja Selection Exam, Orochimaru launches *Operation Destroy Konoha.* Lord Hokage sacrifices his life to halt the attack; in the aftermath, Tsunade steps up to become the Fifth Hokage. Meanwhile, charmed by the power of Orochimaru, Sasuke defeats Naruto and departs Konoha; struggle as he will, Naruto can do nothing to stop him.

More than two years pass. Naruto and his friends undergo rigorous training. Yet when they finally catch up with Sasuke, his power overwhelms them.

Determined to best Sasuke, Naruto returns for another round of intense training. Meanwhile, Shikamaru and the others violently clash with the Akatsuki group. Though the scene looks grim, Naruto arrives just in time to deliver his lethal attack…

NARUTO

VOL. 38
PRACTICE MAKES PERFECT

CONTENTS

WIND STYLE! RASEN-SHURIKEN!

HERE WE GO!

ZOOOSH

Number 340: The Perilous Bridge

SKF

I'M COMIN' IN!

NO! STEER CLEAR OF NARUTO!
YOU'LL JUST GET CAUGHT UP IN IT!
!

...

SO THIS IS THE POWER OF THE NINE TAILS' JINCHÛRIKI.
THE JUTSU CERTAINLY BEFITS THE BEAST.

ZW
OO
SP
!
AK
SHFF
SH
OOM

SHREE
PFOF
FOFF
FOOM

BWUP
!!
RAAGH!
UNH...

SHH

SPOF

HM?

HUH ...?
DID HE WIN?

...
NO, IT FELL SHORT ...

ALWAYS A BUNDLE OF SURPRISES, THAT BOY... ALL RIGHT.
YAMATO!
FWOO

RIGHT!

YEEG!

SKRUUNK

YOUR HEART BELONGS TO ME.

SHRIK

!

CH IT
HYA!!
FWOSH
GWURR

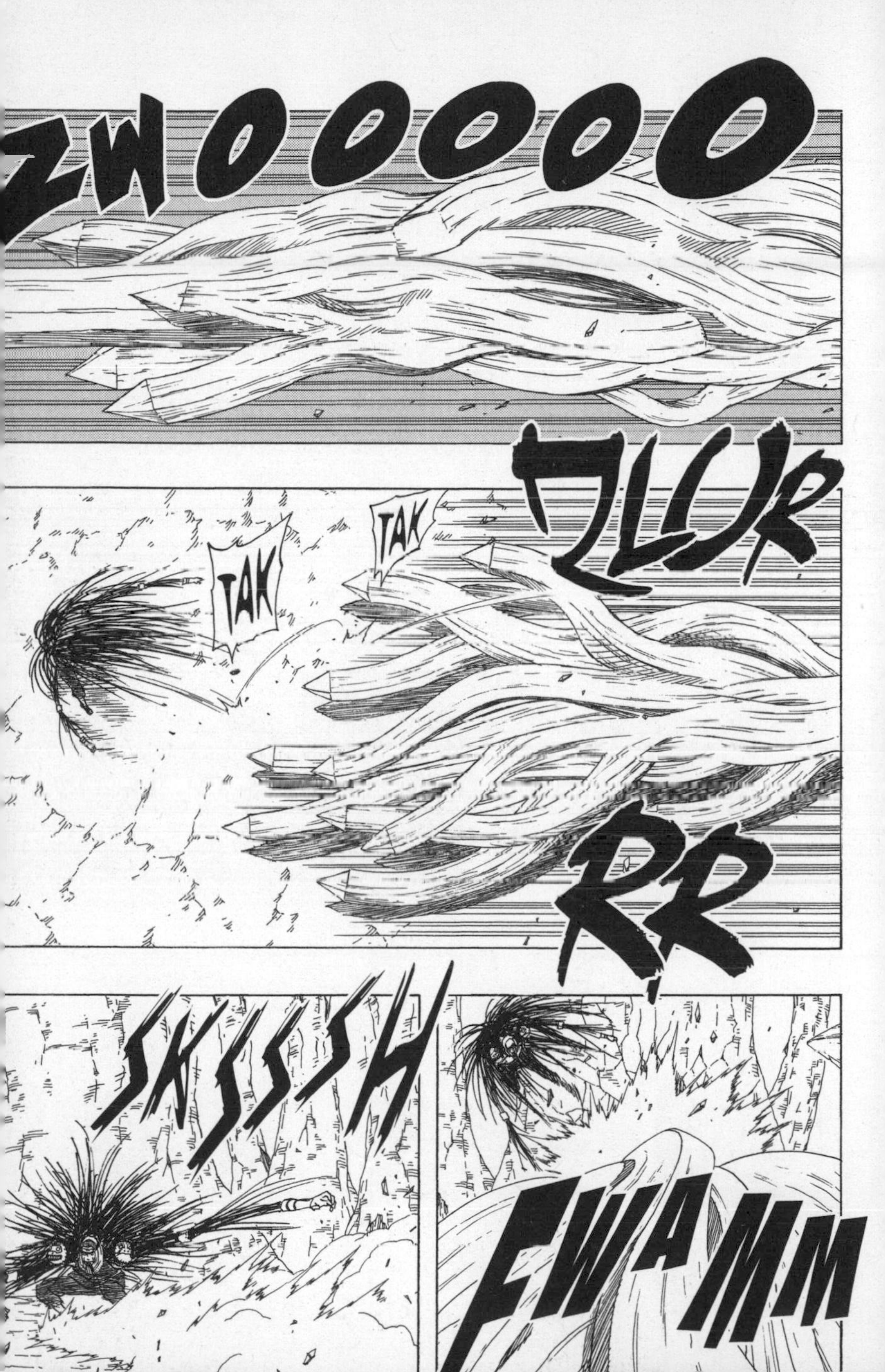
ZWOOOOO
TAK
TAK
FWAMM
SKSSSH

OH MAN!!
...

YOU SEEMED DIFFERENT, NARUTO. BUT I GUESS...
YOU'RE STILL THE SAME OLD NARUTO AFTER ALL.

WHEN YOU SAID *RASEN-SHURIKEN*, I FIGURED YOU'D BOOM-ERANG IT.
DO YOU REALLY NEED TO RUN UP AND SMACK HIM HEAD-ON?

HEY! IT'S AWESOME WHEN IT HITS, OKAY?!

HMM ...

READ
THIS
WAY

...

YEAH, THE NAME IS MISLEADING. RASEN-SHURIKEN ONLY REALLY WORKS AS A MELEE ATTACK.
ZWOOP
THUS THE NEED FOR A DIVERSION. THUS ALL THE SHADOW DOPPEL-GANGERS.

THIS NEW JUTSU BURNS TOO QUICKLY.
IT LASTS ONLY A FEW SECONDS.

THEN WE'RE STUCK. WE CAN'T HIT HIM THAT FAST.
NOT THIS GUY...

LOOKS LIKE HIS JUTSU IS USELESS... SO LONG AS I KEEP MY DISTANCE.
SO, AVOID CLOSE COMBAT AND KEEP MY EYE ON THE REAL BODY. OKAY, SIMPLE ENOUGH.

SFF

LEMME TRY THIS AGAIN.

READ THIS WAY

MASTER KAKASHI.

?

YOU SAID I'M THE ONLY SHINOBI WHO WILL SURPASS THE FOURTH HOKAGE.
AND YOU MEANT WHAT YOU SAID.

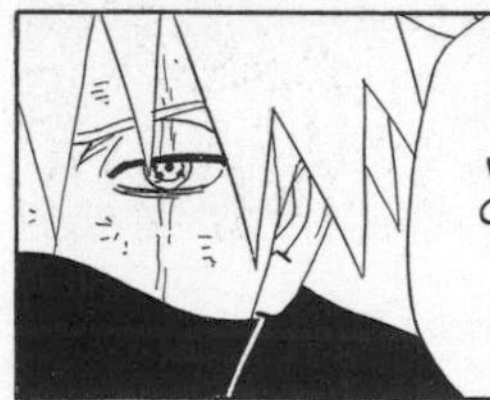

DON'T TAKE AWAY MY CHANCE TO PROVE WHAT I CAN DO!

Number 341: Practice Makes

READ THIS WAY

GO ON, NARUTO.

ALL RIGHT!

...
I'D BETTER SHIFT TO A LONG-RANGE STYLE...

SWOOF
URG...

SPLORT

SPLOOOF

...
WOW...

HE DIDN'T JUST TRANSFORM... THAT'S A LOT OF CHAKRA.

HE'S PREPARING FOR NARUTO'S JUTSU.

FWI
KAGE-BUNSHIN NO JUTSU! ART OF THE SHADOW DOPPELGANGER!!

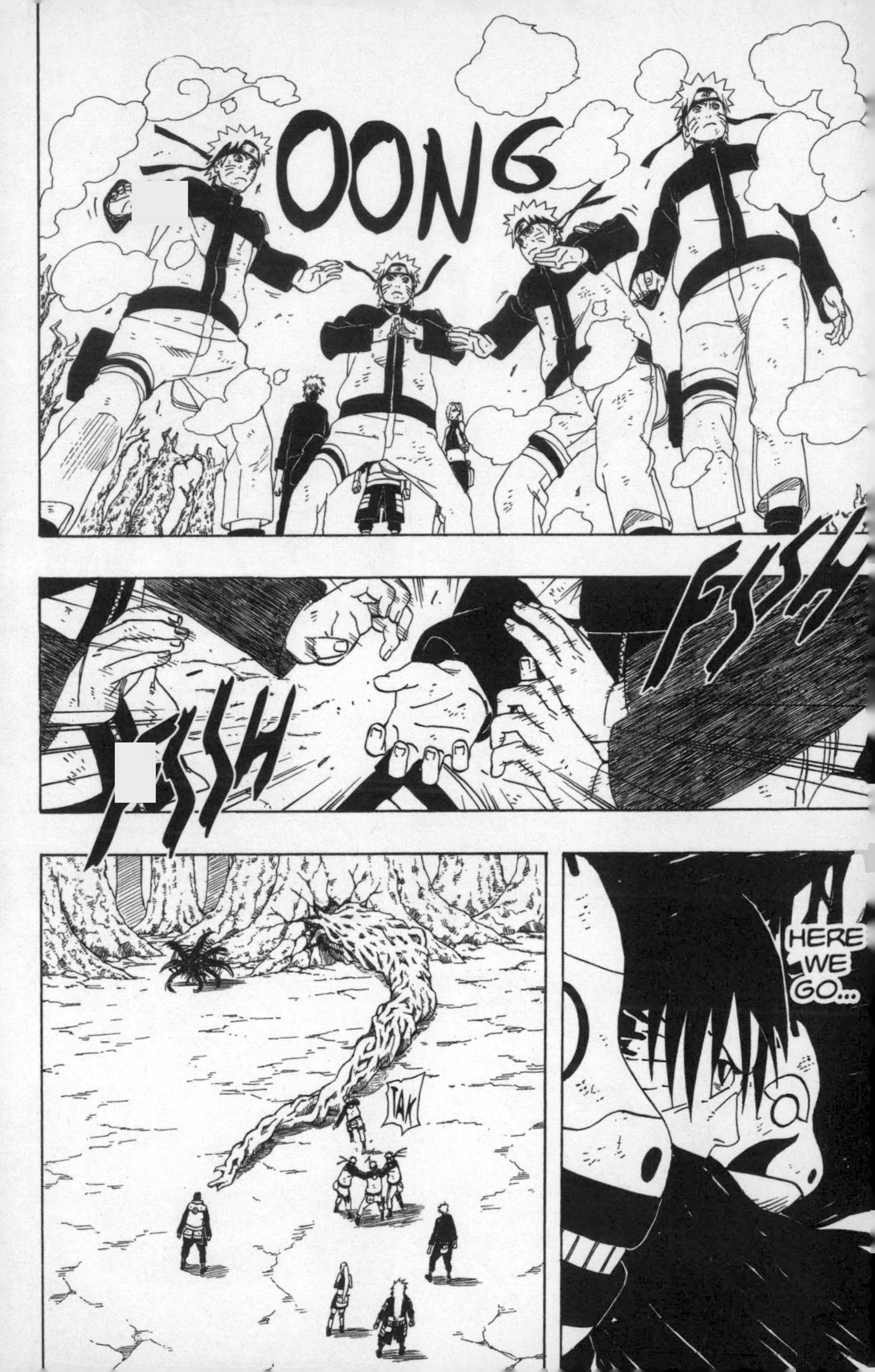
OONG
FSSH
FSSH
HERE WE GO...
TAK

OKAY, NOW!
FWO
FOL-LOW ME!
TAK
SH
SHK
ZOOOSS
SH

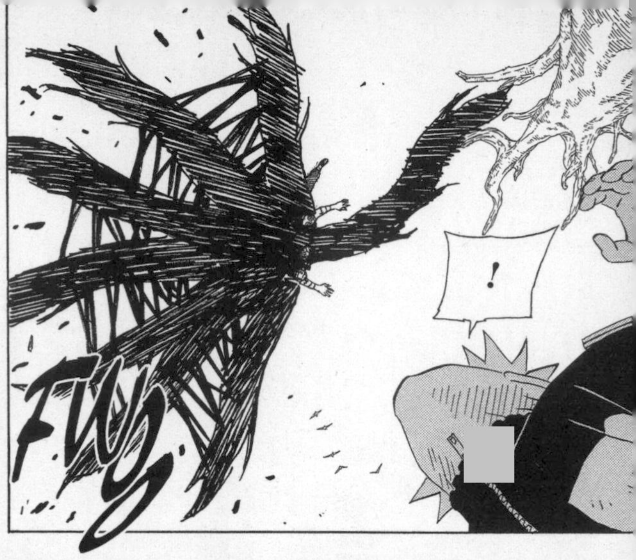
!
FWOSH

WHAT A JUMP!

IGNORE THE DOPPEL-GANGERS. THEY'RE JUST A DISTRAC-TION.
AIM FOR THE HEAD, AND THE REST COMES DOWN.
ONCE I DIFFUSE HIS JUTSU, I'M HOME FREE.

HE'S READY, JUST LIKE I SAID!
ZWOOOM
KOOM

WHAT?
JUST A DOPPEL-GANGER?

POFF

READ
THIS
WAY

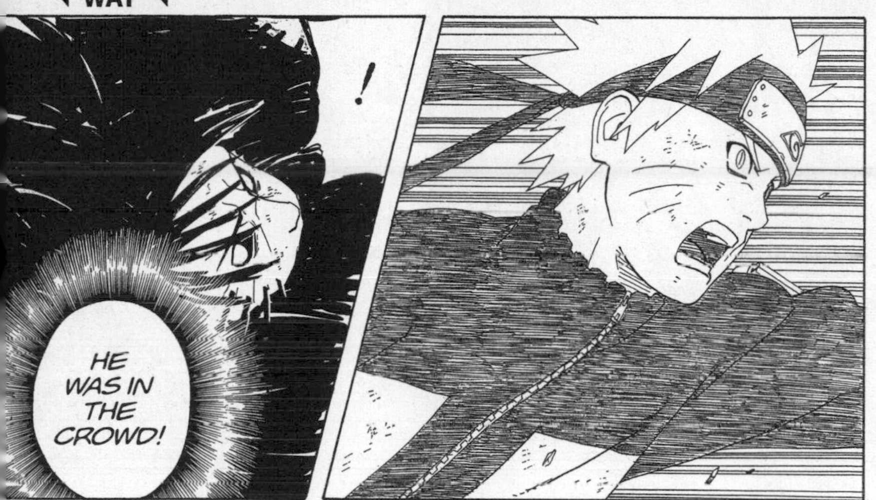
!
HE WAS IN THE CROWD!

GOTCHA!

URGH.

PAKOOSH
VWEE

RUMM MM BLE
GR
ACK!
R
GWURM
FWAP

READ THIS WAY
NGAAH!!

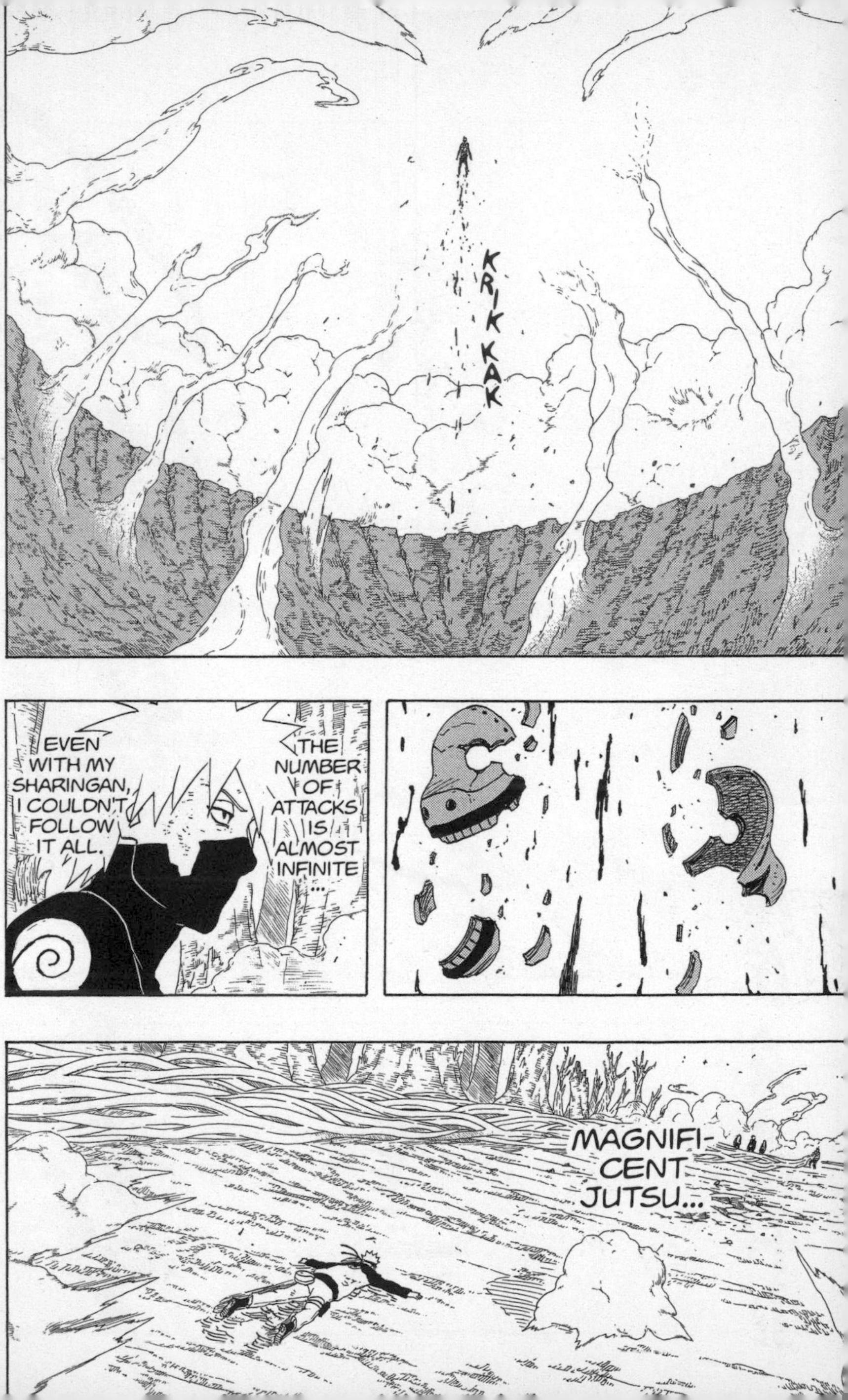

KRIK KAK

THE NUMBER OF ATTACKS IS ALMOST INFINITE...
EVEN WITH MY SHARINGAN, I COULDN'T FOLLOW IT ALL.

MAGNIFI-CENT JUTSU...

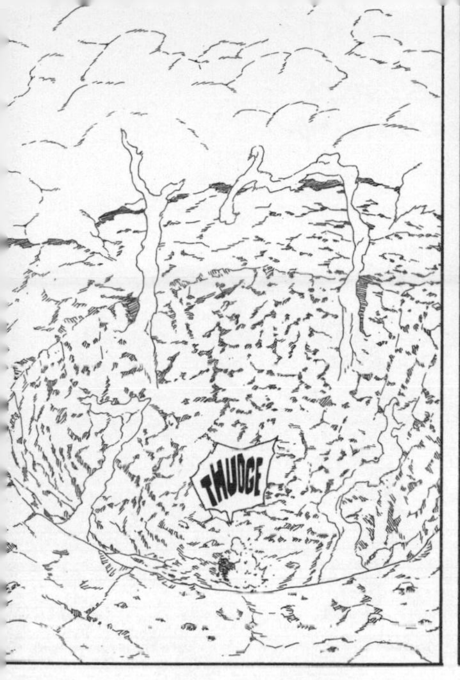
THUDGE

HEH. SWEET.
I DID IT...

MEET KISHIMOTO MASASHI'S ASSISTANTS

○PART 10 ASSISTANT NO. 10: SATÔ ATSUHIRO

[PROFILE]

- ○ A VETERAN OF ULTRA HIGH-PROFILE PROJECTS LIKE *ROOKIES* AND *DEATH NOTE*.
- ○ ONE OF THE FIRST FIFTY PEOPLE EVER TO FINISH HUDSON'S *BOMBERMAN*, AND HAS THE CERTIFICATE TO PROVE IT!
- ○ LOVES VIDEO GAMES AND KNOWS A BUNCH ABOUT THEM. AN EXPERT AT *STREET FIGHTER II*
- ○ ZANGIEF – GIVE HIM AN OPENING AND HE'LL WHIRL YOU AROUND AND BEAT YOU IN AN INSTANT.
- ○ BLANKA – GIVE HIM AN OPENING AND HE'LL ZOOM AT YOU LIKE A CORKSCREW AND KNOCK YOU OUT.
- ○ WOLF – SHOW HIM A WEAKNESS AND HE'LL SPIN YOU AND SLAM YOU DOWN. BUT... WELL, HE'S STILL NEW AT *VIRTUA FIGHTER*.
- ○ INCREDIBLY SKILLED AT ASSEMBLING PLASTIC MODELS (I.E., GUNDAM). HE'S JUST A DEXTEROUS GUY IN GENERAL!

Number 342: The Black King...!

READ THIS WAY

SHK

TEP
TEP

!
FOUND YOU!
TAK

REIN-FORCE-MENTS?
WELL, YOU'RE A BIT LATE.

WHAT?! SHIKA-MARU...
YOU DIDN'T TAKE DOWN AN AKATSUKI ON YOUR OWN, DID YOU?
I DIDN'T KNOW YOU WERE THAT GOOD.

SST

I HAD TO. THIS TIME, I...I KNEW I JUST HAD TO.

READ THIS WAY

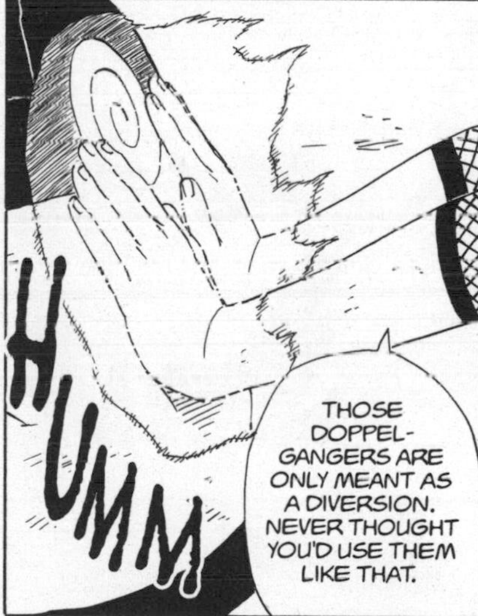
HUMM
THOSE DOPPEL-GANGERS ARE ONLY MEANT AS A DIVERSION. NEVER THOUGHT YOU'D USE THEM LIKE THAT.

HEH...
NOT QUITE AS DUMB AS YOU LOOK, NARUTO. NOT IN SHIKAMARU'S LEAGUE, BUT HEY.

PLEASE DON'T COMPARE ME TO SHIKA-MARU...

I'M IMPRESSED. YOU PULLED OFF THAT JUTSU THREE TIMES IN A ROW.
YOU COULD ONLY DO IT TWICE DURING TRAINING.

...

SUCH CONFIDENCE... AND THE WIT TO TURN FAILURE ON ITS HEAD AND QUICKLY PLAN HIS NEXT MOVE.

NARUTO HAS BECOME STRONG. TRULY STRONG.
JUTSU THAT WERE BEYOND EVEN THE FOURTH HOKAGE ARE WELL WITHIN HIS COMMAND.

I GUESS IT'S TIME TO PASS THE TORCH...
HE HAS SUR-PASSED ME.

...
CAN YOU SENSE IT?

READ THIS WAY

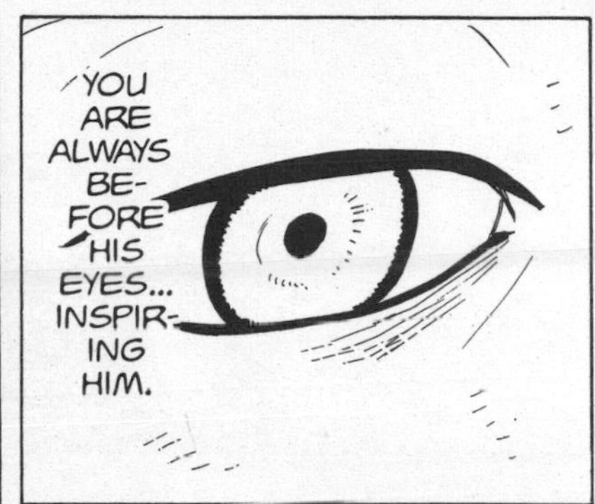

OKAY, PEOPLE. WE'RE MOVING BACK TO KONOHA.
SHF

WHAT ABOUT MASTER KAKASHI?
HE'S CLEANING UP.

TAK
URK...

DE-FEATED ...BY A BUNCH OF ...BRATS ...

READ THIS WAY

WELL... YOU DID FIGHT THE FIRST HOKAGE.
I GUESS I CAN'T BLAME YOU FOR SEEING US AS KIDS.
BUT IT GOES TWO WAYS. TO OUR EYES, YOU'RE JUST AN OLD GEEZER GONE WRONG.

AND HERE YOU ARE DYING, HUGGING THE EARTH LIKE A WORM.
BZZZAK
ONE BY ONE...
THE NEW GENERATION WILL CATCH UP TO YOU. AND THEY WILL ALL SURPASS YOU IN THE END.
BZZZA
SPAK

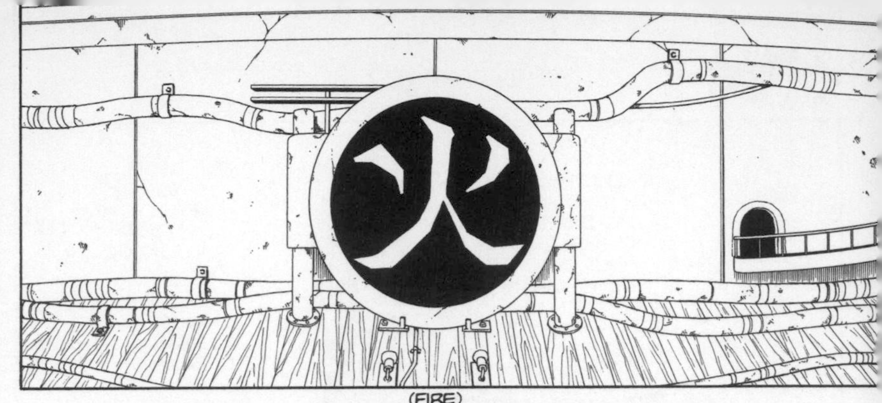

(FIRE)

WELL DONE, PEOPLE.

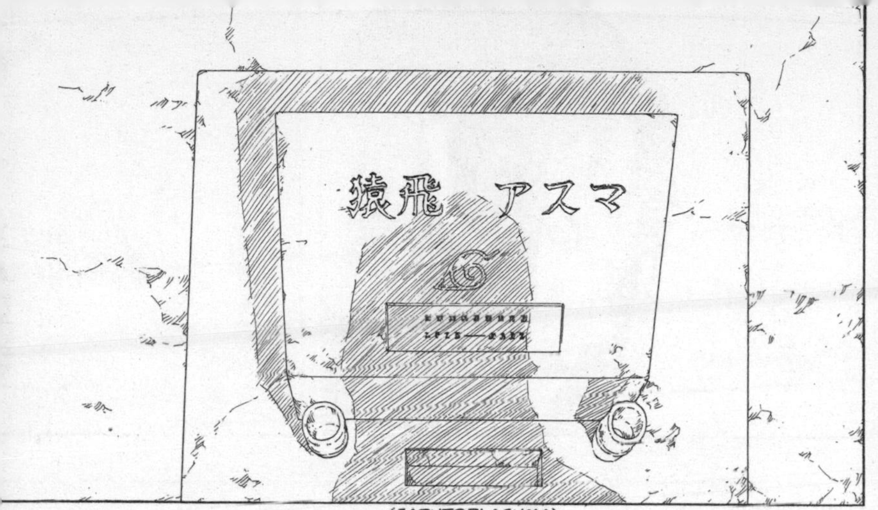

(SARUTOBI ASUMA)

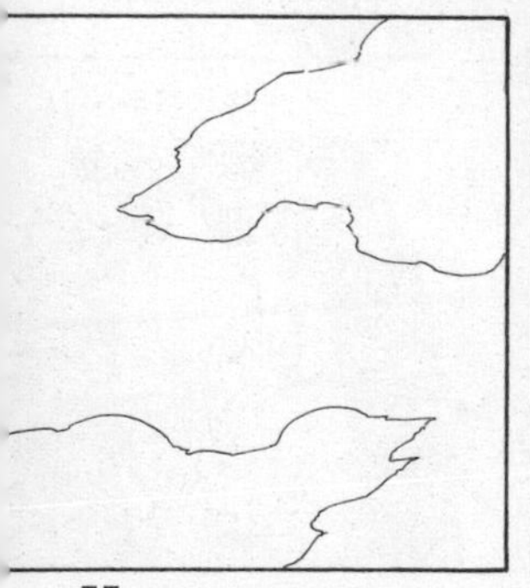

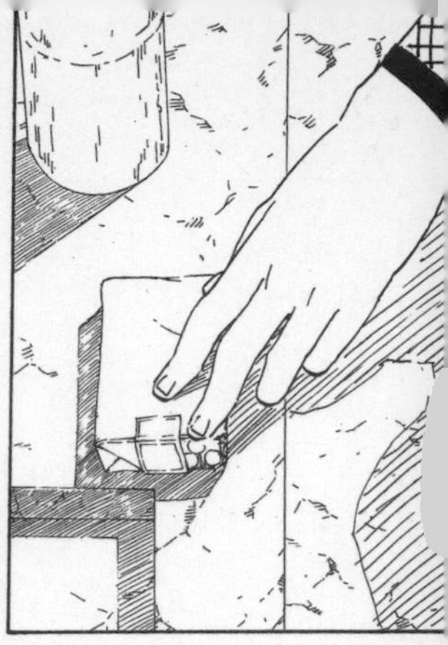

YOU LOST YOUR SHOGI MATE...
YOU WERE ASUMA'S FAVORITE.
YOU MUST MISS HIM TOO...

HE TAUGHT ME A BUNCH OF THINGS... SOME MORE IMPORTANT THAN OTHERS.
SHOGI WAS ONE OF THEM.

IF I SAID I DIDN'T MISS HIM, I'D BE LYING.
BUT I'M NOT A KID ANYMORE, AND I'M EXPECTED TO ACT MY AGE.
I CAN'T DO THE SELF-PITY THING.

...

...
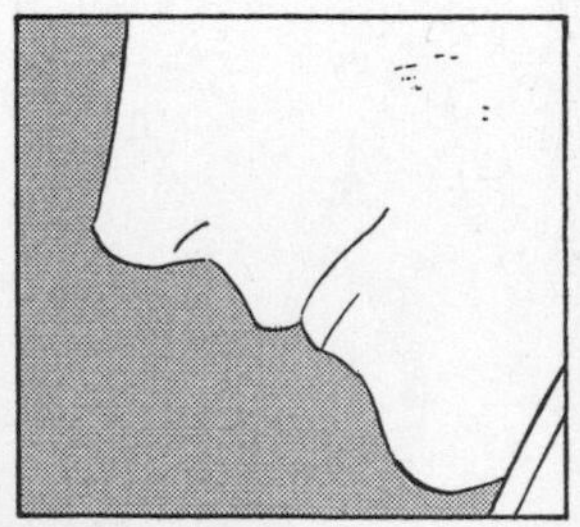

READ THIS WAY

I... I USED TO COMPLAIN ABOUT EVERYTHING. EVERYTHING ANNOYED ME BACK THEN.
I MADE SO MANY MISTAKES BECAUSE OF IT.
AND EVERY TIME, ASUMA CAME TO MY RESCUE...

HE WAS AN ODD TEACHER...
SO ELUSIVE... SO HARD TO FIGURE OUT.
猿飛 アスマ

BUT TO ME, HE WAS STILL A TERRIFIC ROLE MODEL.

SHF
AND NOW IT'S MY TURN.

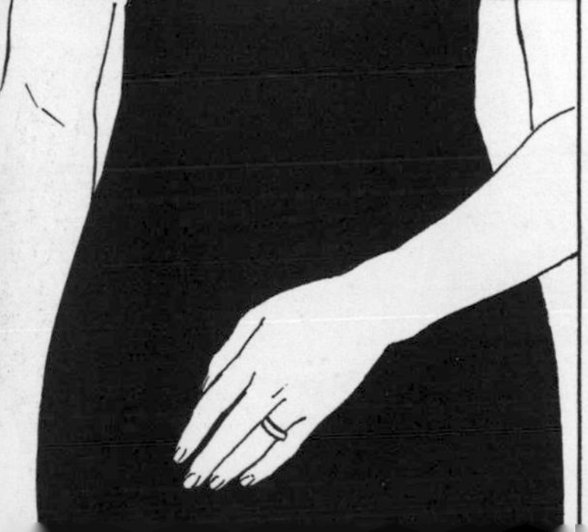

WHEN THAT BABY ARRIVES...
IT'LL BE MY TURN AS GUARDIAN AND MASTER.

READ
THIS
WAY

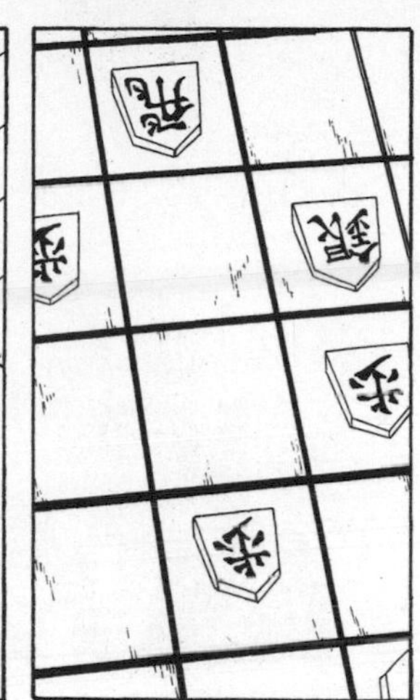

DAD, YOU'RE MUCH BETTER AT THIS THAN ASUMA.

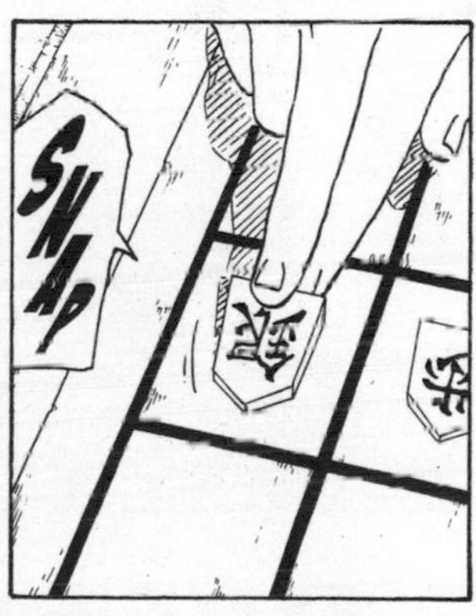
SNAP

CLIMB-ING SILVER, EH?
SNAP

WELL, YOU KNOW. WHEN DEFENDING THE BLACK KING AGAINST A STRONGER OPPONENT ...
SACRIFICE IS UNAVOID-ABLE.

LOOK, IF YOU RETREAT THAT WAY...
MY KNIGHT CAN BARREL RIGHT UP HERE.
SNAP

AND NO MATTER WHICH OF MY GOLD GENERALS GETS AWAY, YOUR BISHOP WILL ENTER AND BE PROMOTED ...
BOY, THAT'S ONE DEVIOUS KNIGHT YOU'VE GOT THERE.

IF KONOHA'S SHINOBI WERE SHOGI PIECES...
THAT WOULD BE ME.

WHAT'RE YOU TALKING ABOUT?
IT'S SOMETHING ASUMA SAID ONCE.

...

DID HE... I GUESS HE KNEW YOU INSIDE OUT.
SNAP
THAT HE DID.

王
SNAP

SO THEN... WHO'S THE BLACK KING?

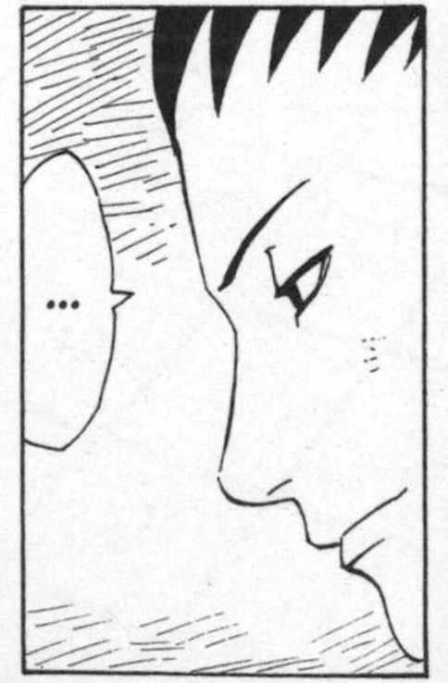
...

...

THE CHILDREN WHO WILL CARRY KONOHA ON THEIR SHOULDERS.
THEY'RE THE BLACK KING.

YOU DO GET IT, DON'T YOU.
AND... CHECKMATE.

AH!

YOU'RE NOT YET STRONG ENOUGH TO PROTECT THE BLACK KING!
YOU NEED TO WORK HARDER!
ARGH!

THOK

DID I GET THEM ALL?
AWG!
UNGH!

ERF...

AND NOT A SINGLE FATAL BLOW.
YOU'RE STILL TOO SOFT-HEARTED.

THEY'RE NOT THE ONES I'M SETTING OUT TO KILL.

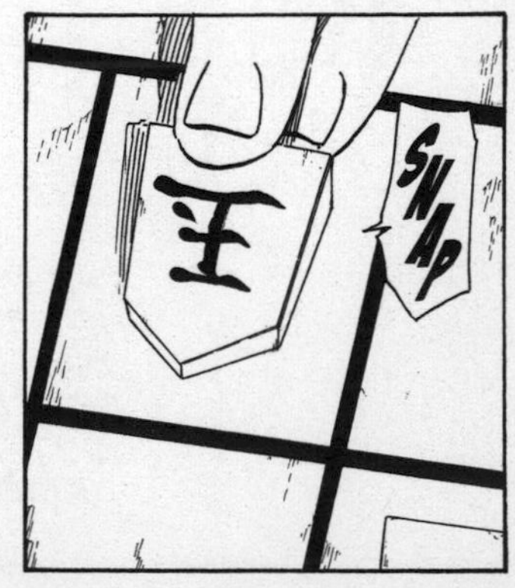
SNAP

Number 343: Merciless...

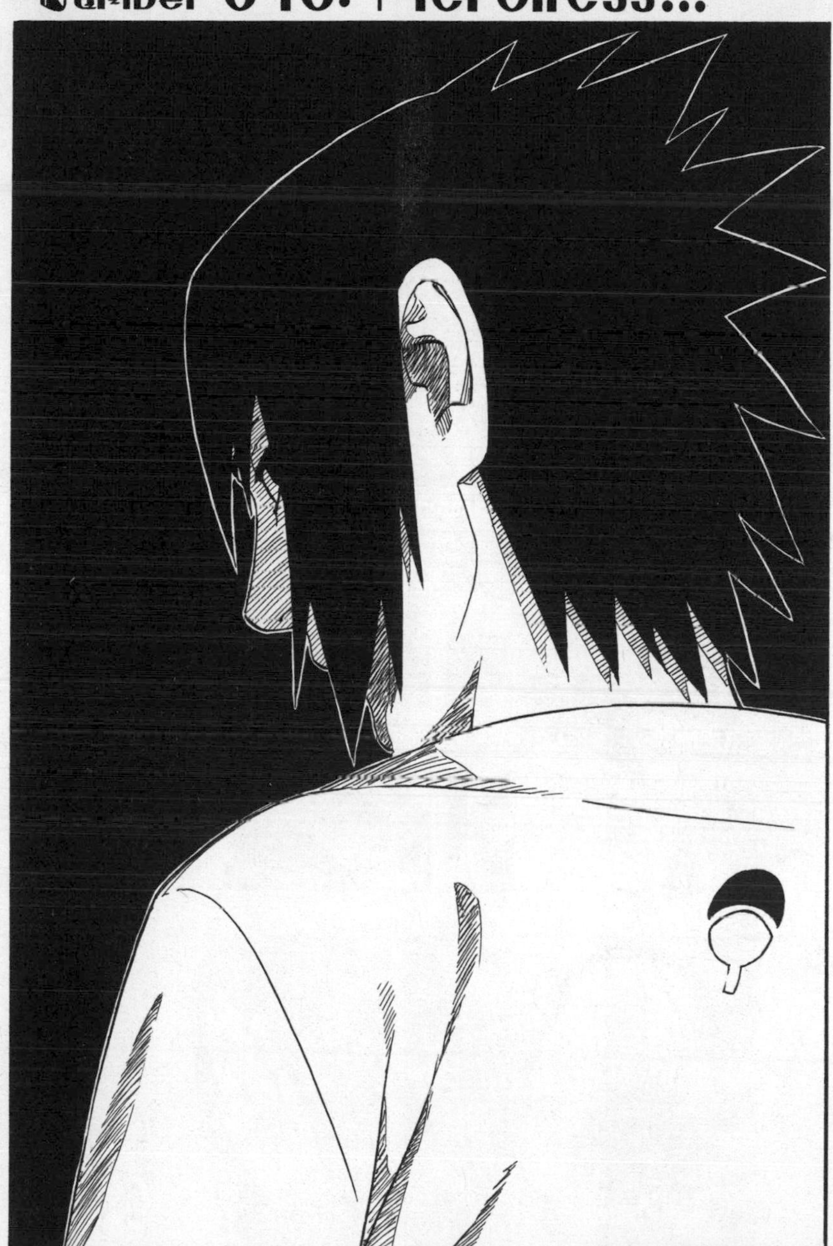

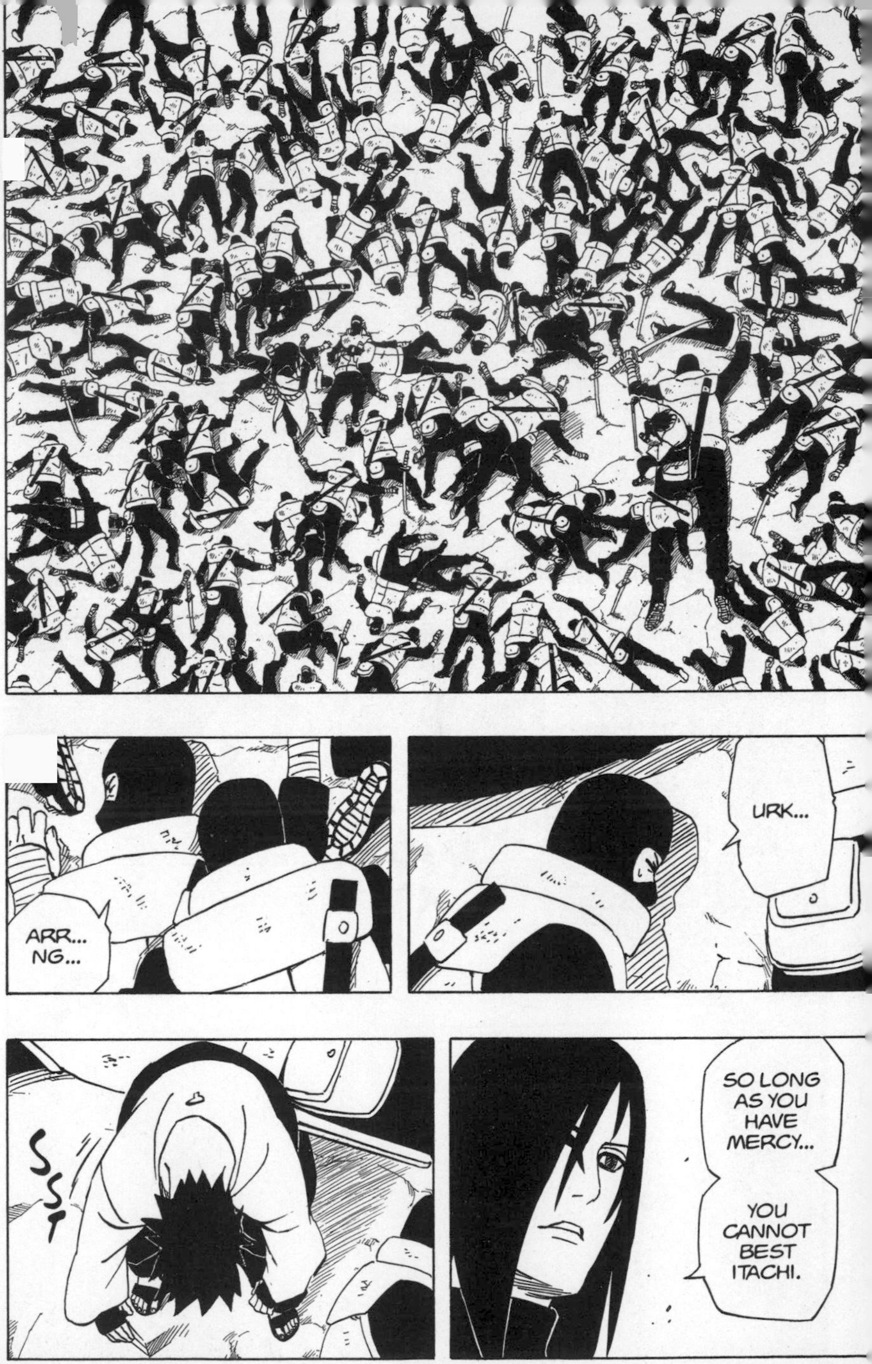

URK...

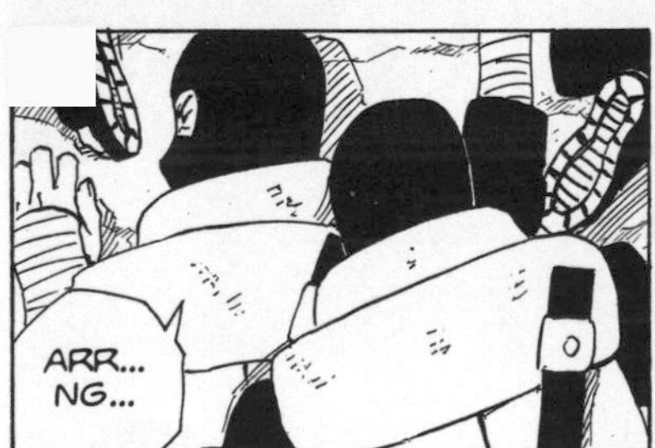
ARR... NG...

SO LONG AS YOU HAVE MERCY...
YOU CANNOT BEST ITACHI.

SST

READ THIS WAY

I'LL BE MERCILESS ENOUGH WHEN I SEE HIM.
THAT WON'T TAKE ANY EFFORT.

SPOK

TAK

NOT A DROP OF BLOOD ON HIM...
THEY CALLED ME A GENIUS, BUT COMPARED TO HIM...

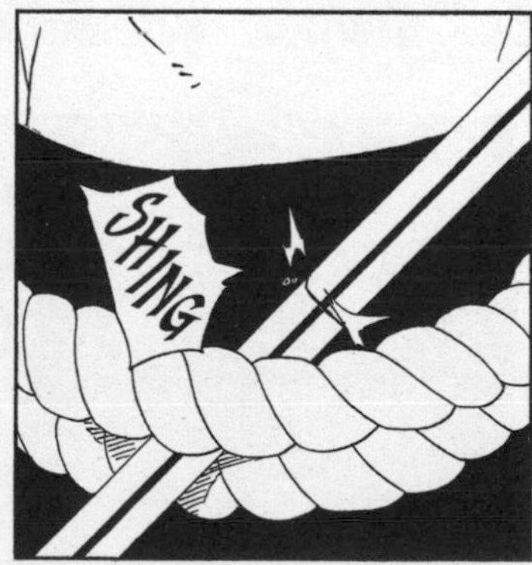
SHING

TEP
TEP

JUST A LITTLE LONGER...
A LITTLE MORE PATIENCE, AND HE'S MINE!

(ICHIRAKU)

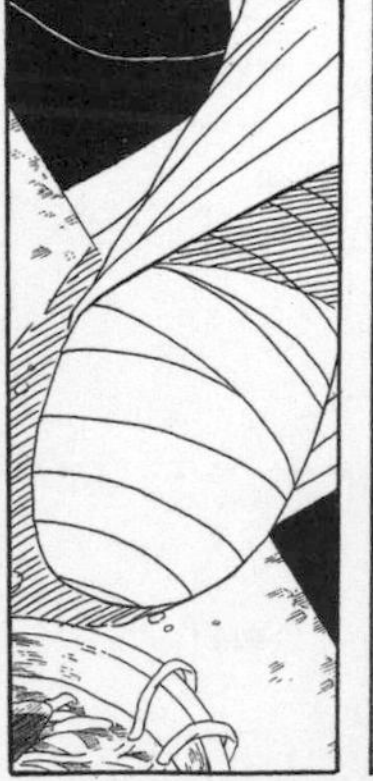

READ THIS WAY
YOU MUST'VE BROKEN HALF THE BONES IN YOUR BODY! IT'S NOT MADE FOR THIS KIND OF STRAIN...
SSS
THIS NEW JUTSU OF YOURS IS ONLY MEANT AS A LAST RESORT!
JUST PROMISE ME YOU'LL THINK BEFORE USING IT!
HEH...HEY, IT'S NO BIG DEAL. SO LONG AS I'VE GOT YOU AROUND TO FIX ME.
THAT'S NOT THE POINT!
THERE ARE LIMITS TO WHAT I CAN PATCH UP! MEDICAL NINJUTSU IS A SCIENCE, NOT A MIRACLE CURE!
...
YEAH, STILL... I LIKE THINGS THE WAY THEY ARE NOW.
HUH?

'CAUSE, SAKURA, IT FEELS LIKE WE'RE ON THE ROAD TO REACH SASUKE TOGETHER.
SKRRT
YOU'RE HOPE-LESS.
GIMME YOUR CHOP-STICKS.
!
AM I DREAMING? SHE'S NOT GOING TO...
...FEED ME?

NOW SAY AH... ♪
TWIKK
HOT!!!
IT'S TOO HOT!! AND WHO ASKED FOR YOUR HELP?!
ZWIP

MASTER KAKASHI, HOW ARE YOU EVEN OUT OF BED?
WHY DOES EVERYONE KEEP ASKING THAT?
HMPH.

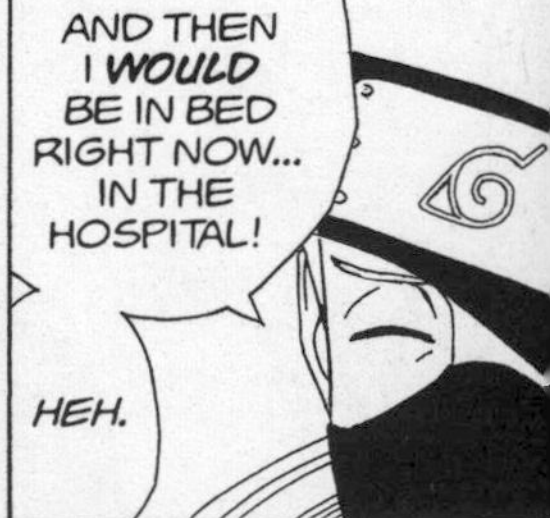

READ
THIS
WAY

YOU'RE STRONG, NARUTO.
YOU MAY EVEN SURPASS ME.

THING IS, THE MORE PROFOUND THE JUTSU...
...THE RISKIER IT IS TO WIELD. JUST REMEMBER THAT.

YEAH...

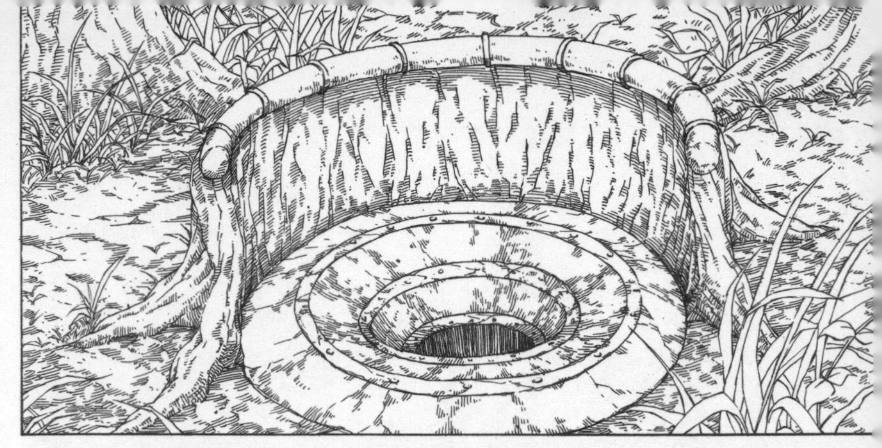

KAFF
KAFF
YOUR BODY HAS REACHED ITS BREAKING POINT.
IF YOU DON'T TAKE THE LEVEL-10 MEDICINE, THERE'S NOT MUCH MORE I CAN DO FOR YOU.

HAA
HAA

SHK
I'LL GO GET THE OTHER MEDICINE.

CREAK
I'LL BE RIGHT BACK.
B-TUM

READ THIS WAY

HEH...
HA HA HA HA HA HA HA.

...

HA HA...
KAFF
KAFF

!

SHK
FWSSH

READ THIS WAY

THIS CHAKRA ...
I'VE NEVER SEEN IT CHANGE ITS FORM LIKE THIS.

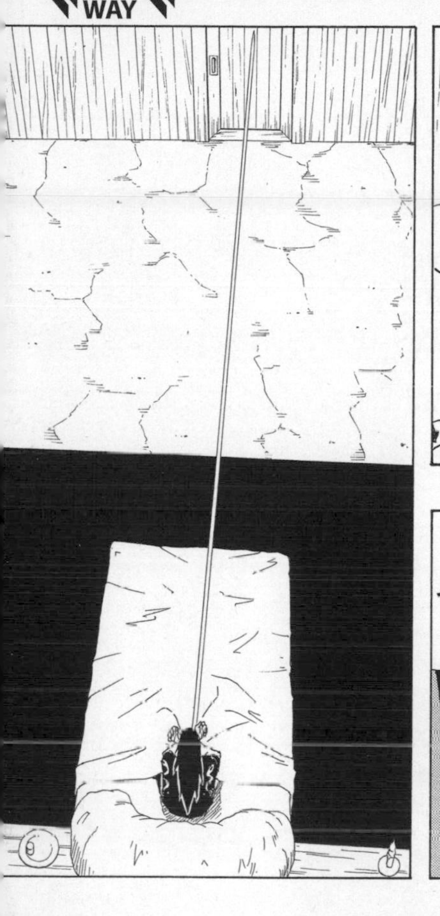

WHO'S THERE?

SPA KKAK

CHU KKA

READ THIS WAY

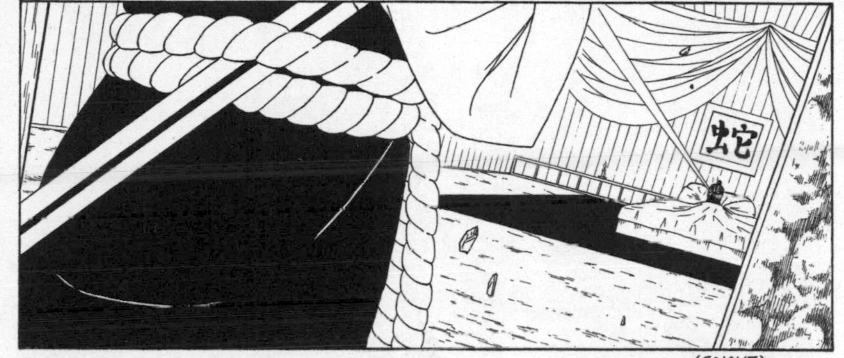

(SNAKE)

MEET KISHIMOTO MASASHI'S ASSISTANTS

○ PART II ASSISTANT NO. 11: SHIRASAKA AKIO

[PROFILE]

○ GREW UP WAY OUT IN THE BOONDOCKS, SO WHEN ASSISTANT NO. 9 (MURAKAMI) STARTS GABBING ABOUT COUNTRY LIFE, HE CHIMES IN WITH GUSTO.

○ PERPETUALLY QUIET, HIS LIPS CURLED UP INTO A PLEASANT SMILE—CAUSING ASSISTANT NO. 6 (TASAKA) TO KEEP REPEATING, "I CAN'T FIGURE HIM OUT! WHAT'S HE THINKING?!"

○ WANTS TO DRAW MANGA, BUT TOO ENTRANCED WITH THE GAME *MONSTER HUNTER* TO STOP PLAYING, LEADING TO TROUBLE WITH ASSISTANT NO. 8 (ITAKURA).

○ HE IDOLIZES ASSISTANT NO. 3 (IKEMOTO) LIKE A BROTHER. THAT'S BECAUSE THEY SHARE THE SAME PASSION FOR *MONSTER HUNTER*.

○ HE'S A WHIZ AT DRAWING, AND THAT'S

Number 344: The Snake...

OROCHIMARU.

I'M STRONGER THAN YOU.

READ THIS WAY

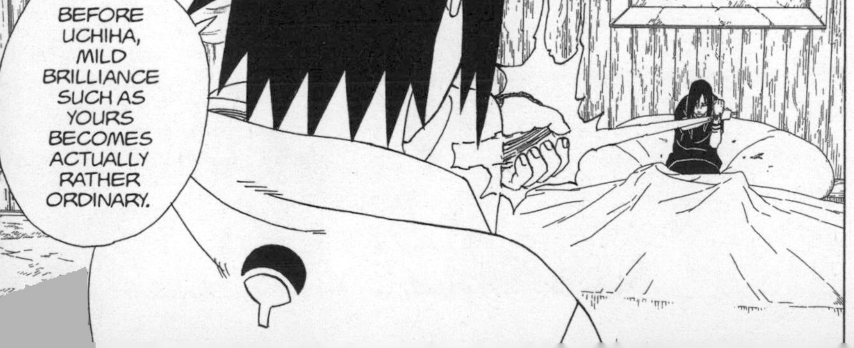

FILLING YOURSELF UP WITH MEDICINES, LEAPING FROM BODY TO BODY...
AND THE WAY YOU COVET THE POWER OF UCHIHA ...IT'S REVOLTING.

AS AN UCHIHA, ALL I SEE IS A MISERABLE WRETCH.

AND ANYWAY, I DON'T LIKE YOUR STYLE.
I MEAN, WHAT ARE YOU AFTER?

UNLOCKING THE MYSTERIES OF NATURE?
YOU KEEP TOYING WITH PEOPLE, ALL FOR THIS VAIN AND FRANKLY STUPID CAUSE OF YOURS.

READ THIS WAY

WHY...
...DID YOU...?

TO MEASURE MY CAPACITY.

MEASURE YOUR CAPACITY ...
THAT'S IT...?
THAT'S... THE ONLY REASON FOR KILLING... EVERY-BODY?

I HAD TO.

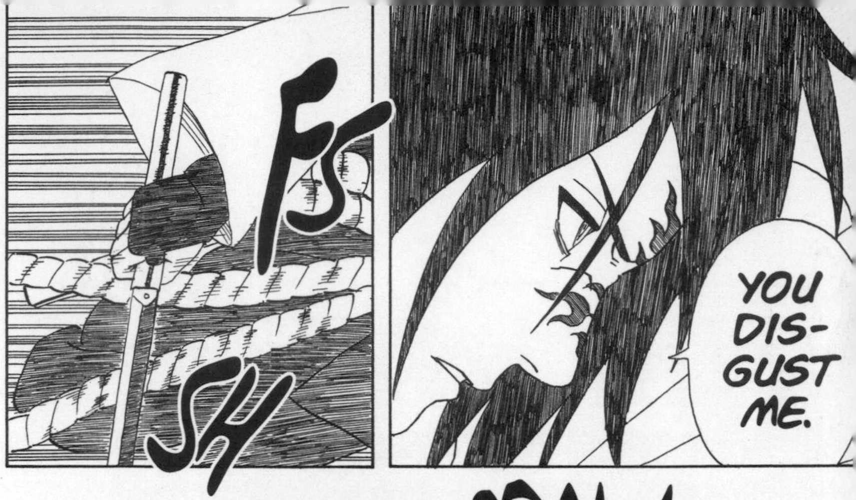
FSSH
YOU DIS-GUST ME.

SPAKKAKKA

SHAA

SPOP
WSSH
SPLOOT
!
CHOK
PLISH

TO CHANGE BODIES...
YOU EXPERIMENTED ENDLESSLY.

NOW... SASUKE... YOU ARE MINE...

GIVE ME YOUR BODY!!

FWOOSH

PA

FWOOOSH

HSSSSS!

SKRRT

ZWOOF

SHF

CHINK

SHIK

FZUP

SHWAP

HAA
HAA

ZWURR RRRR

!

SKLORCH

DLAP

PLSP

...

...THE SNAKE IS PREY BECAUSE THAT BIRD IS A HAWK...

READ THIS WAY
... READY TO TAKE TO THE SKY!
...
SASUKEEE!!

!

WHAT IS THIS?

OH! THAT'S THE SKIN OF A WHITE SNAKE. WHAT LUCK THAT YOU FOUND IT.

I'VE NEVER SEEN ONE OF THESE BEFORE.
HEH... ME NEITHER.
THEY'RE EXTREMELY RARE. NOT TOO MANY GET THE OPPORTUNITY.

WHY IS IT SO WHITE?

WHO KNOWS. IT'S NOT IN THE BOOKS.
I DON'T THINK ANYONE'S BOTHERED TO LOOK INTO IT.

ALL I KNOW IS THAT THE WHITE SNAKE IS A SYMBOL OF GOOD LUCK AND RENEWAL.

IT MUST BE KARMA FOR YOU TO FIND IT HERE BY YOUR PARENTS' GRAVESTONE. MAYBE IT MEANS THEY'VE BEEN REBORN SOMEWHERE?

HEY, MAYBE SOMEDAY YOU'LL MEET THEM AGAIN.

NARUTO

Number 345: The Ritual...!!

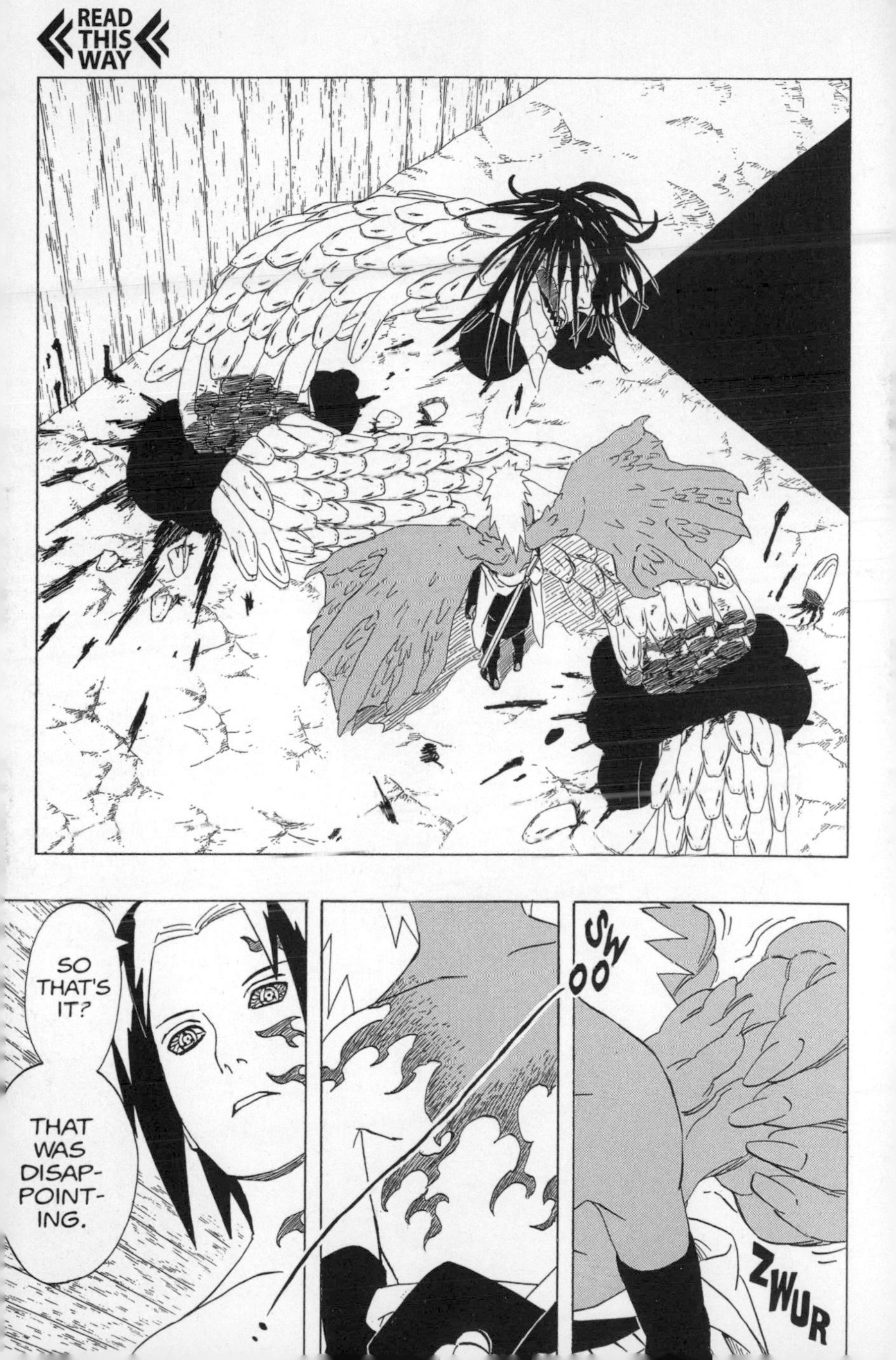

SWOO
ZWUR
SO THAT'S IT?
THAT WAS DISAPPOINTING.

?
WOOOP

URK...

IT'S ABOUT TIME IT TOOK EFFECT.

THE BODILY FLUIDS OF THE GREAT SERPENT WILL EVAPORATE THE MOMENT THEY'RE EXPOSED TO THE AIR.
THEY HAVE... A NUMBING EFFECT.
ZWUP

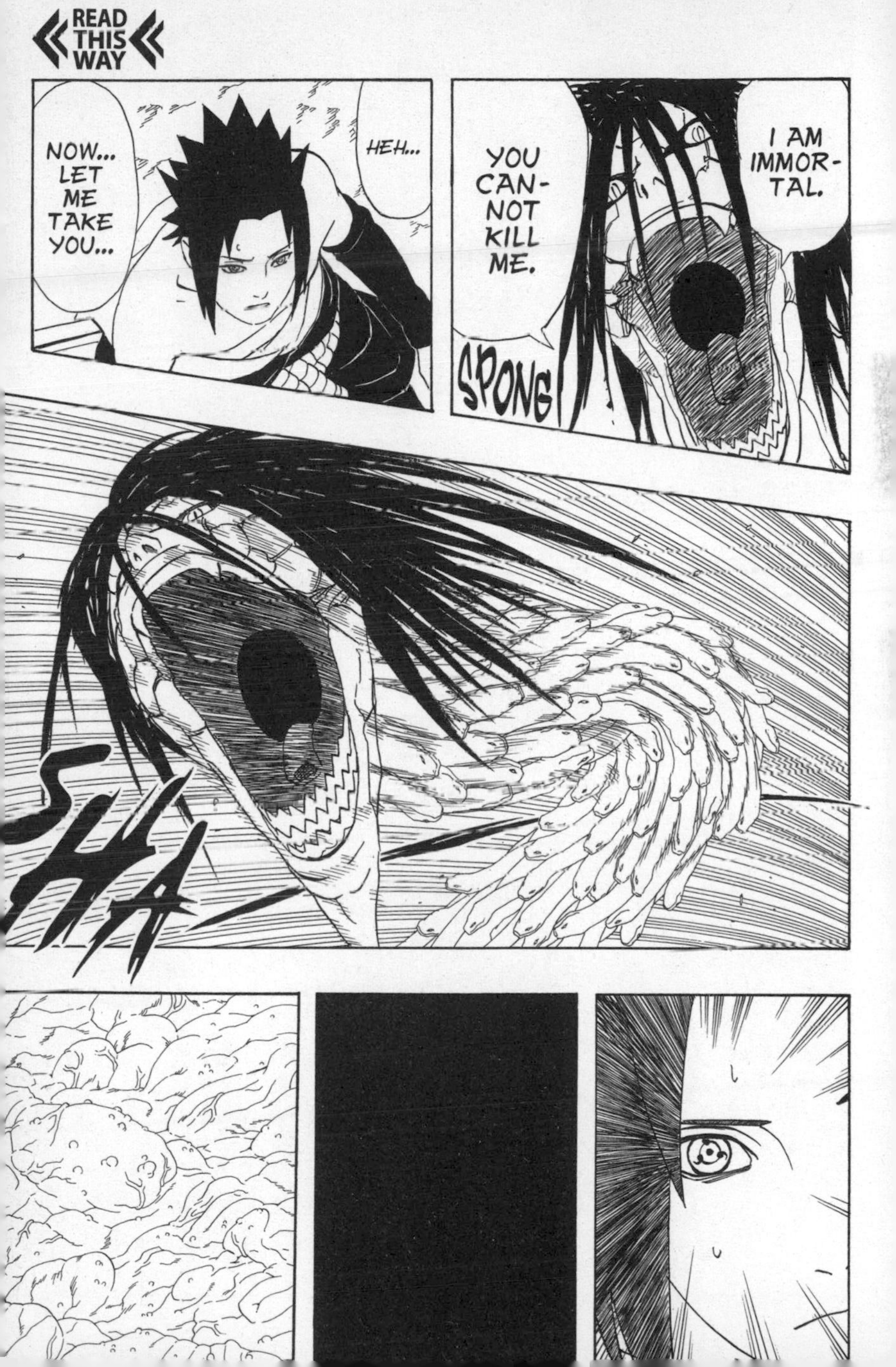

READ THIS WAY

I AM IMMORTAL.
YOU CANNOT KILL ME.
SPONG

HEH...
NOW... LET ME TAKE YOU...

SHA

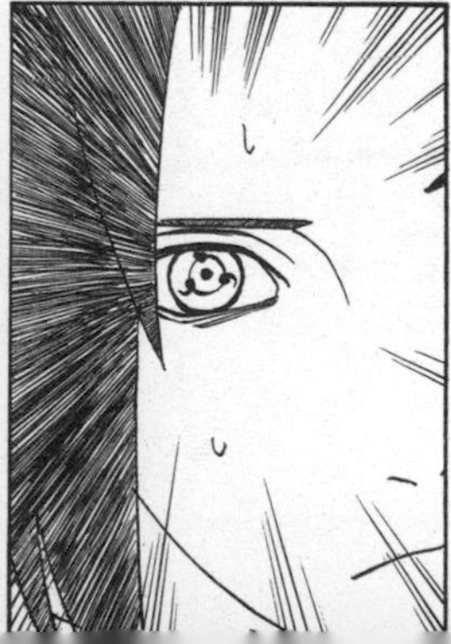

WHAT IS...
...THIS PLACE?

MWORMWOR
THIS IS THE UNIVERSE INSIDE OF ME.
THIS IS WHERE THE TRANSFERENCE RITUAL TAKES PLACE.

...

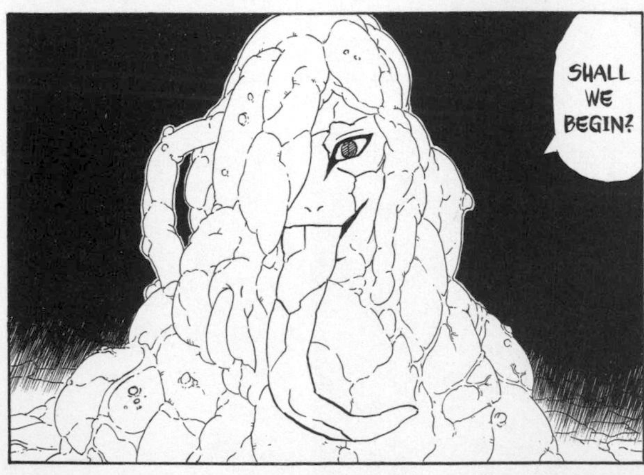
SHALL WE BEGIN?

READ
THIS
WAY

!
ZWUP

!

!

ZWURR

HOW CAN THIS BE POSSI-BLE...
HOW CAN THE GENJUTSU PARALYSIS BIND ME...
WHAT STRONG EYES YOU HAVE.
MAGNIF-ICENT.

READ THIS WAY

TWIK TWIK

OROCHI-MARU, MY EYES...
...CAN SEE THROUGH YOUR JUTSU.

IT'S AS IF I'M LIVING THAT MOMENT ALL OVER...

HEH... HEH HEH...
AND THOSE EYES...
THEY'RE FINALLY MINE!!

READ THIS WAY

NO MEDICINE WILL HELP HIM NOW.
TOMOR-ROW...
OR BETTER, TODAY. THE SOONER WE PERFORM THE RITUAL, THE BETTER.

...

I CAN'T IMAGINE SASUKE WILL GO ALONG WITHOUT A FUSS...

SHK

STILL, IT'S NOT LIKE HE COULD DO A THING ABOUT IT. NOT AGAINST THAT RITUAL...
HEH...

G-CHAK

B-TUM

!

...

ZOOSH

SKF

SST

!

WHY IS HE HERE?!

READ
THIS
WAY

THE GIANT SNAKE HAS SHED ITS SKIN...
SO... HAS THE RITUAL ALREADY TAKEN PLACE?

WHAT'S GOING ON?!

KABUTO?

SHF

TCP

SST

READ THIS WAY

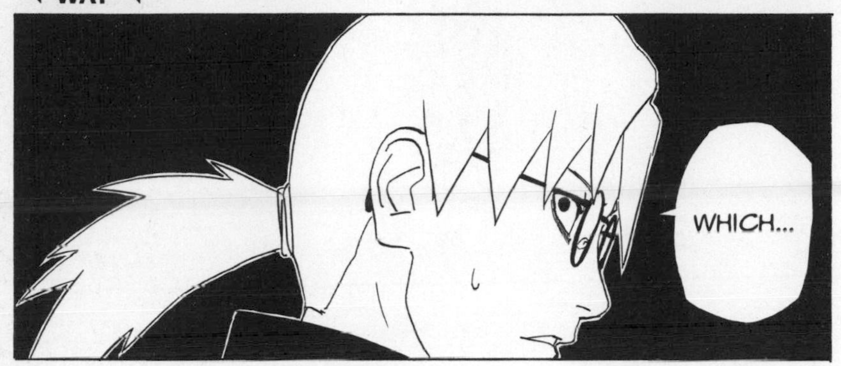

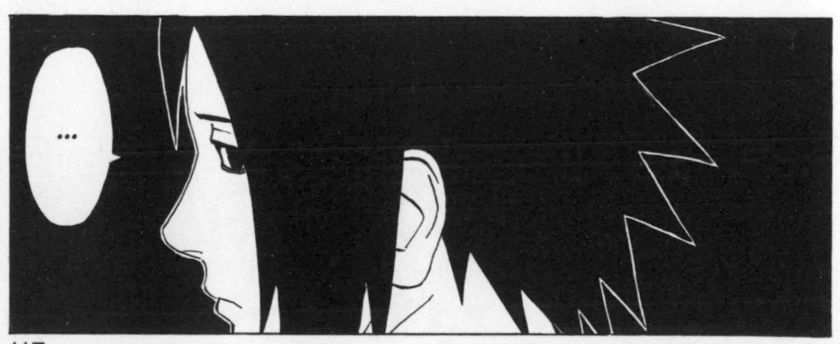

NARUTO

Number 346: The Secret of the New Jutsu!!

WHICH DO YOU THINK?
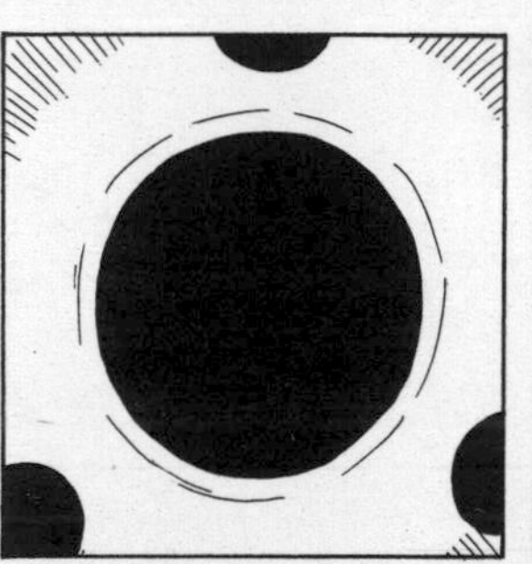
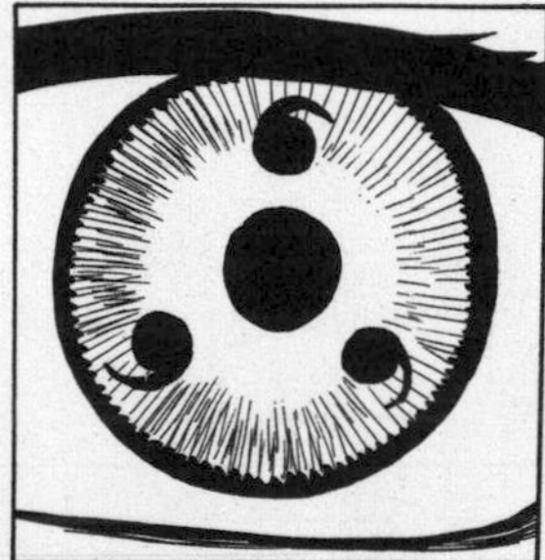

SWOO-...

!

!

IT'S THE RITUAL...
ZWUR

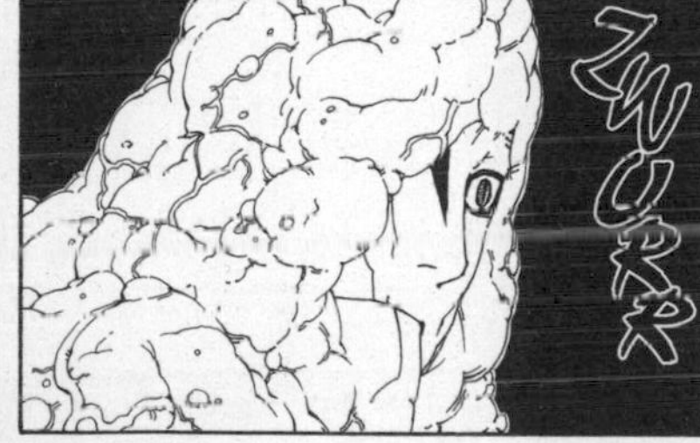
ZWURR

ZWURR

ZWUR

ZWURRR

?!

SHOOM

ZWUR
ZWUR
ZWUR

?!

READ THIS WAY

CHOMP
...!
THIS ...
CHOMP

ZWURRRR
NO...NO! THIS IS MY UNIVERSE! I CREATED IT!
THIS CAN'T HAPPEN!

IT CAN'T!
IT'S IMPOS-SIBLE!
THIS IS MY OWN SPACE!

OROCHI-MARU, MY EYES CAN SEE THROUGH ALL YOUR JUTSU.

UR RR

SURELY YOU MUST KNOW...

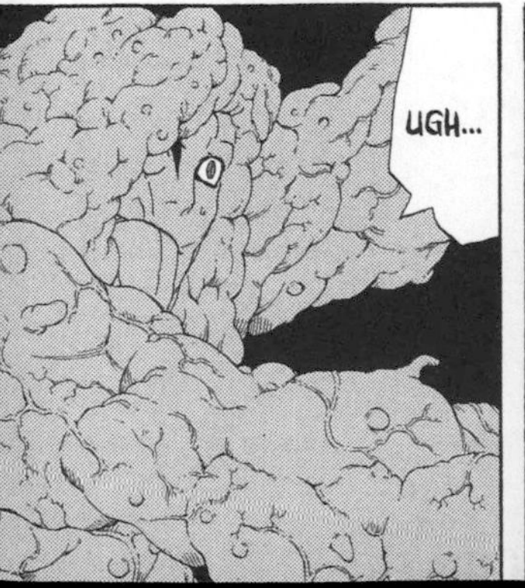

ZW
ALREADY...

THIS CAN'T...
ZWUP
THIS CAN'T BE HAPPEN-ING!

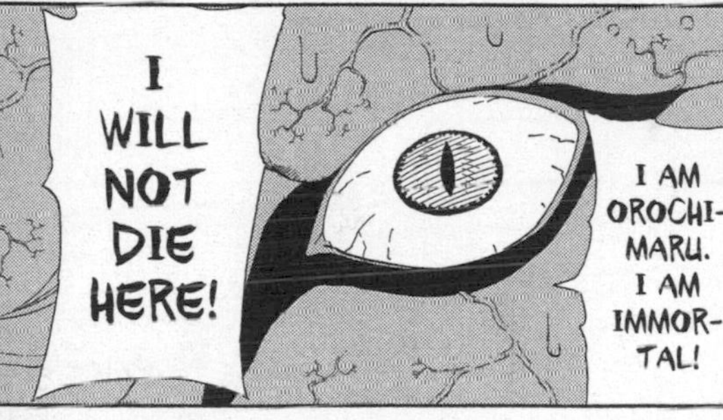
I AM OROCHI-MARU. I AM IMMOR-TAL!
I WILL NOT DIE HERE!

I...I AM THE ONE WHO...WILL UNLOCK THE MYSTERIES OF NATURE!
I AM THE... ONE WHO WILL RECEIVE ...EVERY-THING!!

NO...

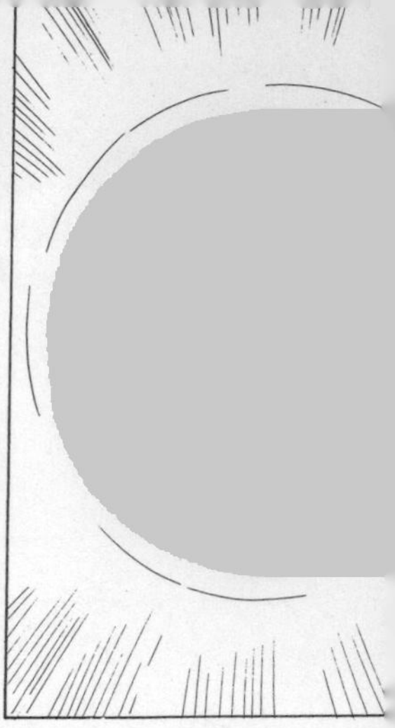

I ABSORBED HIM. THAT'S ALL.

(ICHIRAKU)

HIS CHAKRA NETWORK HAS BEEN COMPLETELY SEVERED.

IT'S HARD TO IMAGINE. BUT IT IS SO.

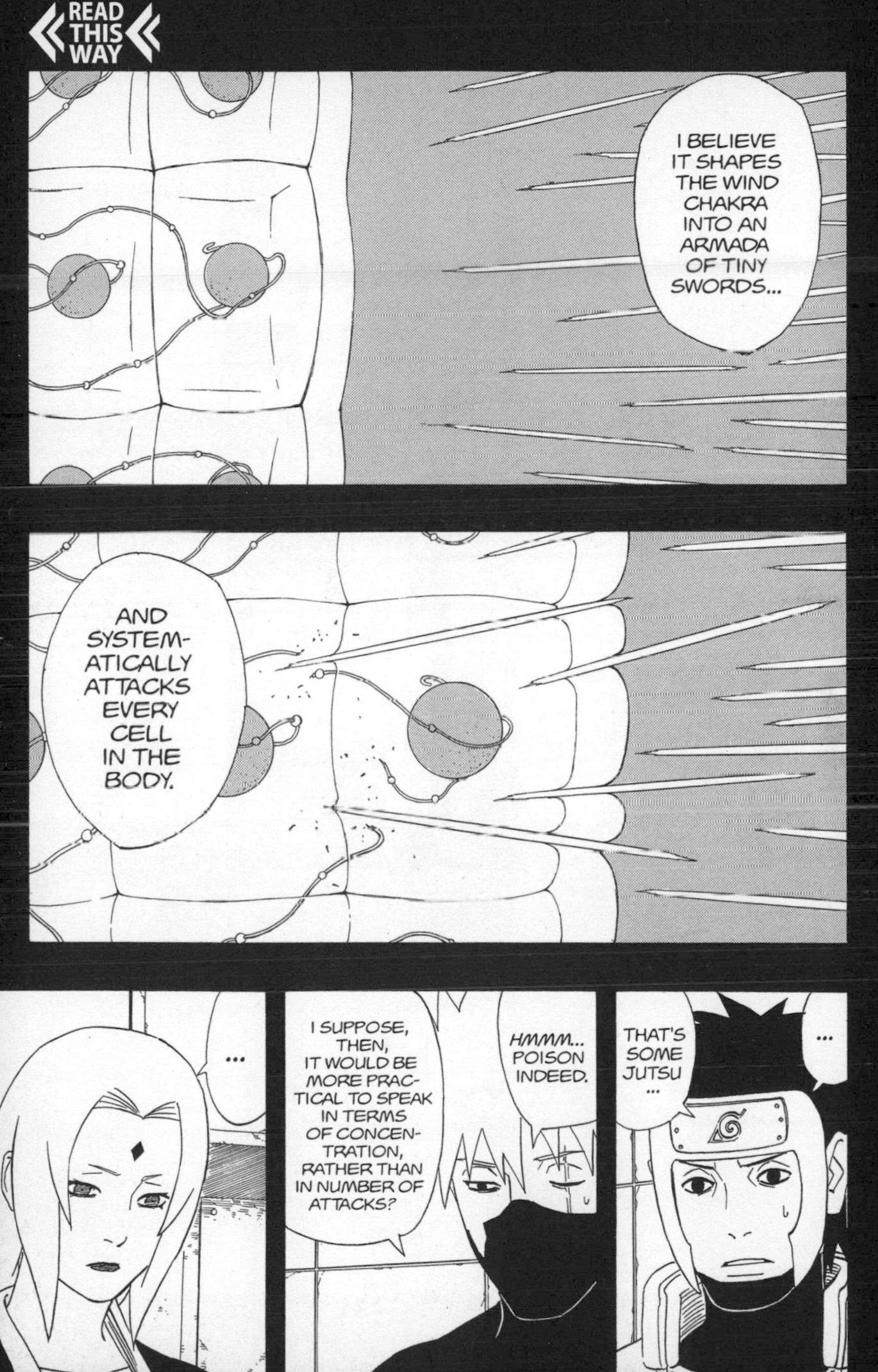
READ THIS WAY
I BELIEVE IT SHAPES THE WIND CHAKRA INTO AN ARMADA OF TINY SWORDS...
AND SYSTEMATICALLY ATTACKS EVERY CELL IN THE BODY.
...
THAT'S SOME JUTSU...
HMMM... POISON INDEED.
I SUPPOSE, THEN, IT WOULD BE MORE PRACTICAL TO SPEAK IN TERMS OF CONCENTRATION, RATHER THAN IN NUMBER OF ATTACKS?
...

SO... HOW'S NARUTO?
賭
WELL ...
THERE'S OUR REAL PROB-LEM.
FIGURED AS MUCH...
...
...
KAKASHI ...
DON'T ALLOW NARUTO TO USE RASEN-SHURIKEN. EVER AGAIN.

READ
THIS
WAY

?!

THAT BAD, HUH.

I SAW THOSE SAME SYMPTOMS IN NARUTO'S RIGHT HAND.

NOT AS SEVERE, GRANTED, BUT THE SAME.

IF NARUTO CONTINUES TO USE THE JUTSU, THEN BEFORE LONG...

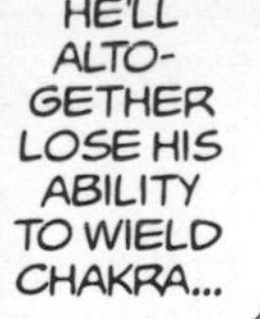
HE'LL ALTO-GETHER LOSE HIS ABILITY TO WIELD CHAKRA...

IT IS A POWERFUL JUTSU...

IT COMES WITH A RISK...

ONCE A CELL OF THE BODY IS CUT OFF FROM ITS KEIRAKUKEI, IT'S BEYOND MY ABILITY TO HEAL IT. EVEN WITH MY MEDICAL NINJUTSU...

BE SURE THAT NARUTO UNDER-STANDS THIS IMPLICITLY.

...

READ THIS WAY

I KNOW HOW I FEEL...
...WAY BETTER THAN ANYONE ELSE DOES!

REMEMBER, I'M GONNA BE HOKAGE!
THAT'S HOW INCREDIBLE I AM! SO DON'T WORRY!

HRRM ...

...

...

THANKS FOR THE FOOD!
IT'S ON MASTER KAKASHI'S TAB!

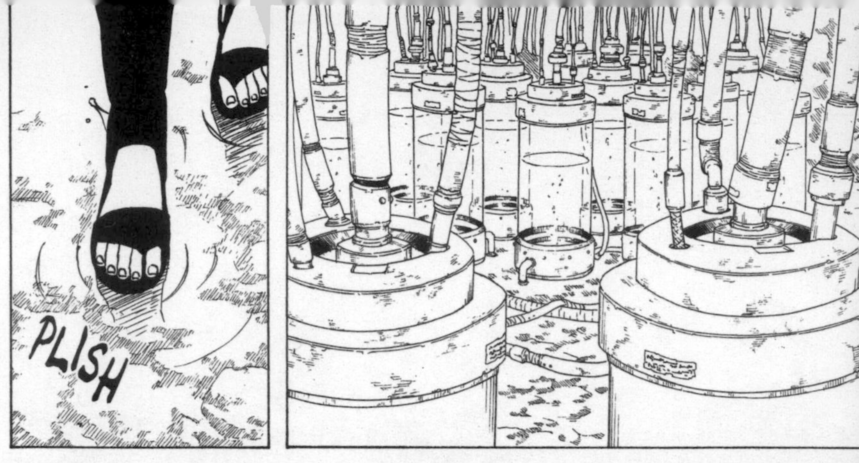
PLISH

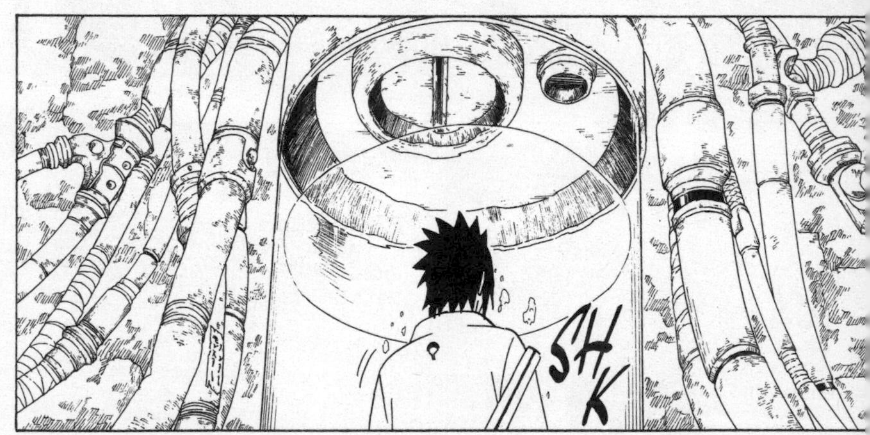
SHK

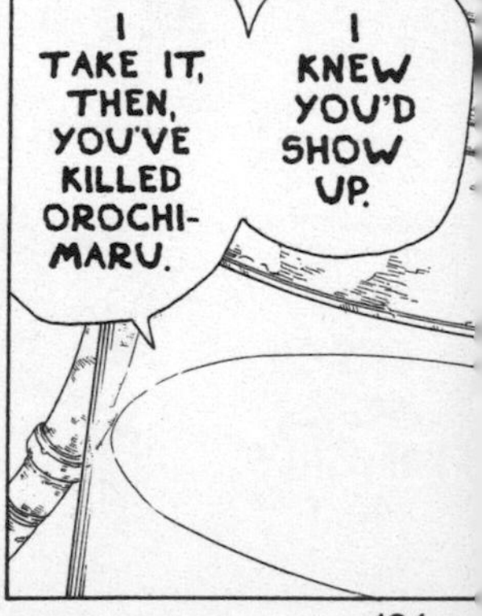
I KNEW YOU'D SHOW UP.
I TAKE IT, THEN, YOU'VE KILLED OROCHI-MARU.

YEAH ...
HERE, LET'S GET YOU OUT OF THAT THING.
SHAK

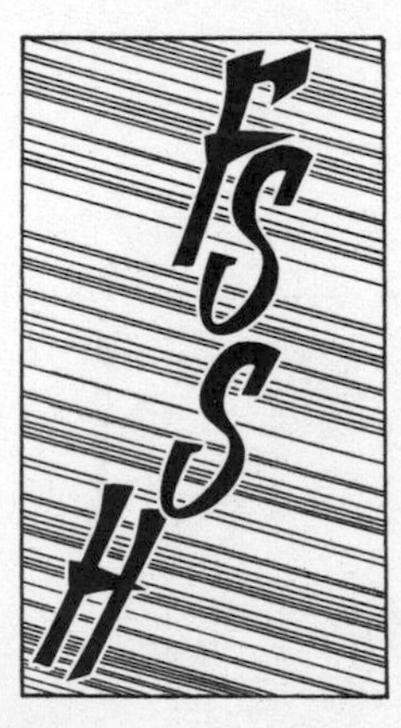
FSSSH

READ THIS WAY

SPOSSH
CHINK

SPLASH

I'M FREE... AT LAST...
SLURR
MY REGARDS, SASUKE.

SUIGETSU ...YOU ARE MY FIRST.
COME WITH ME.

Number 347: A Detour!!

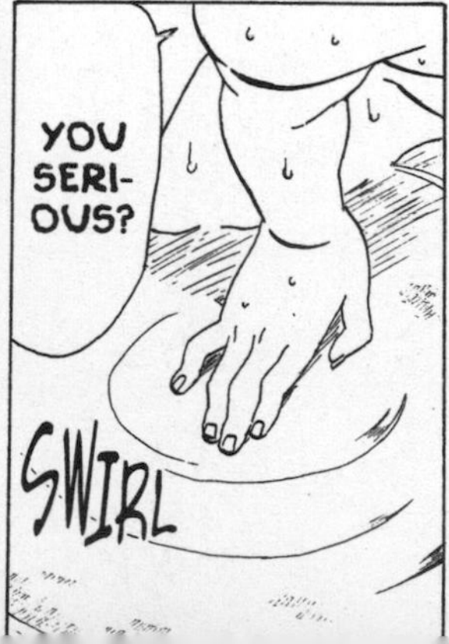

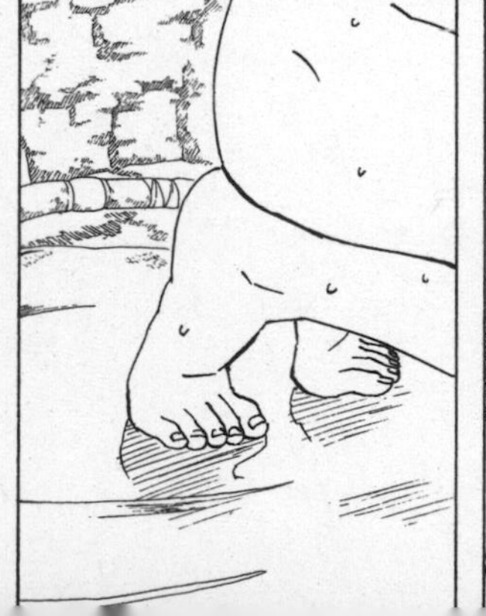

Number 347: A Detour!!

WELL... I'M NOT PARTICU-LARLY FOND OF THEM.

I JUST DON'T THINK WE'D GET ALONG, IS ALL.

READ THIS WAY

YOU DON'T NEED TO BE FRIENDS.
JUST CO-OPER-ATE.

OF COURSE ...AFTER ALL, YOU DID SAVE ME.
IF THAT'S WHAT YOU WANT, I'VE NO OBJEC-TIONS.

STILL, SASUKE, I CAN'T BELIEVE YOU'D GO FOR THEM.
JUST SHUT UP AND GET DRESSED.
WE'RE GOING.

HA HA...
OH DEAR. THE WAY YOU TALK...

FIRST, LET'S CLARIFY OUR RELATIONSHIP...

SHALL WE?

READ THIS WAY

YOU WERE HIS FAVORITE. HE LET YOU STAY BY HIS SIDE WHILE THE REST OF US SLEPT IN CAGES.
YOU HAD ALL THE ADVANTAGE YOU NEEDED.

LOOK AT US TWO. RIGHT NOW, I HAVE THE ADVAN-TAGE.

YOUR POINT IS?

...

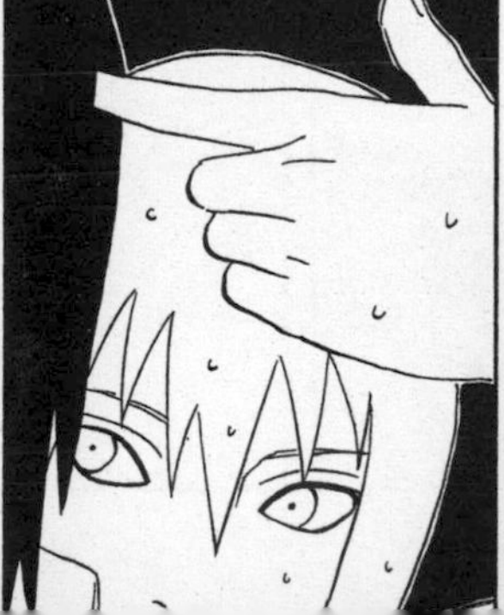

SHF
FORGET IT. JUST TESTING.
THAT WAS A PRETTY BAD SPOT I PUT YOU IN, AND YOU DIDN'T EVEN BLINK.
SO IT WASN'T LUCK, THEN. THAT'S REASSURING.

I'VE HEARD HOW STRONG YOU ARE.

IT WAS YOUR PLATOON, WASN'T IT, THAT TOOK DOWN MY PREDE-CESSOR, MOMOCHI ZABUZA?

...

SURE, I'LL COME WITH YOU.

BUT BEFORE WE GO AND FETCH THE OTHERS...
THERE'S A PLACE I WANT TO SWING BY.

READ THIS WAY

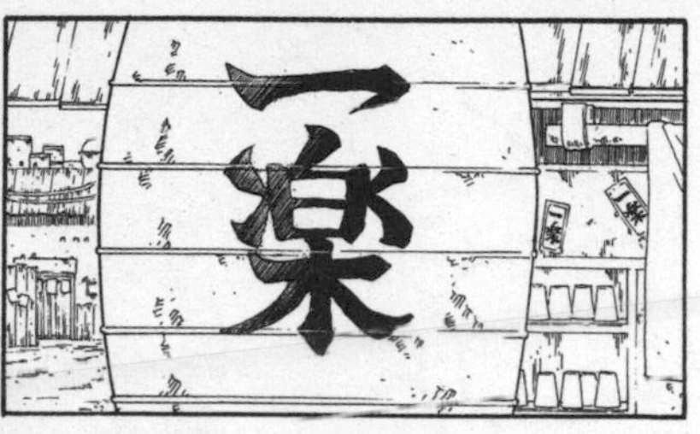

ART OF ONNA-NOKO TACHI!!

AWWWHHH!!

THAT'S YOUR NEW MOVE?!

READ THIS WAY

ZIN
NG
WHAT D'YA THINK OF THAT, NARUTO?!
YOU SEE, WITH TWO GIRLS, IT'S EVEN...
STOMP STOMP

CRUMP
BLARGH!!
SAY NO MORE!
BONG

IS THIS WHAT YOU GUYS DO WHEN YOU GET TOGETHER?!
IS IT?!
ERR... IT'S A FORM OF DIVERSION, SEE...
AND THIS IS A, ERR, SERIOUS PROJECT BETWEEN US TWO...I MEAN, COMPETITION...

WELL, DON'T PUT YOURSELVES OUT!
C'MON!!
DIS-TRACT THE ENEMY?
THE ONLY ONES YOU'LL BE DISTRACTING ARE YOURSELVES !!

FWIP

BONNG

ART OF OTOKO-NOKO TACHI!!

READ THIS WAY

OOP!

SO MAYBE THAT IS TOO MUCH MESSING AROUND...
AWK!
BONK
ON
NG

Y... YEAH...
OKAY, TIME TO LAY OFF THE NEW FANTASY JUTSU, ALRIGHT?
WHY DON'T YOU WORK ON SOMETHING MORE PRACTICAL AND REAL THAN THAT...

!

...
OH... WAIT, I DIDN'T MEAN...
NO, THAT'S NOT... REALLY, I DIDN'T MEAN THAT I...

HEH.
I KNEW IT...!

WHAT'S UP, SASUKE?

(THE GREAT NARUTO BRIDGE)

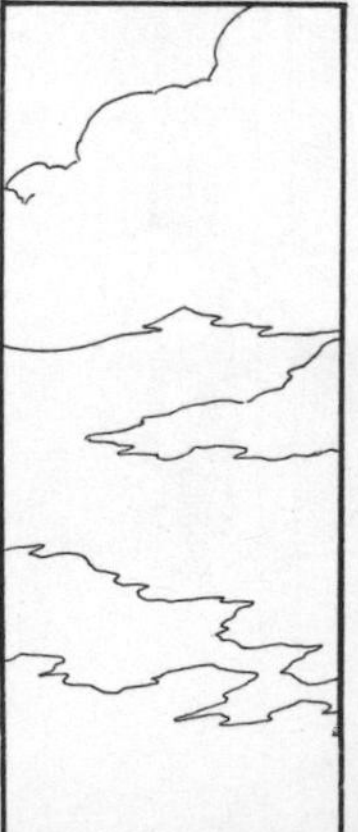

NEVER THOUGHT I'D FIND THIS HERE.
SHK

SORRY, MASTER ZABUZA. THIS IS MINE NOW.
GRIP

SHUNK

PRETTY HEAVY...

THIS IS THE EXECUTIONER'S BLADE, THE SWORD OF THE DEMON ZABUZA FROM THE VILLAGE OF BLOODY MIST.

THE WEAPON OF THE SEVEN NINJA SWORDSMEN HAS BEEN HANDED DOWN, GENERATION TO GENERATION. IT'S THE TRADITION.
AND... ALL THESE YEARS I'VE TRAINED, I'VE DONE IT ONLY OUT OF REVERENCE FOR THE SEVEN NINJA.

SO LONG AS I HAVE THIS SWORD, NOT EVEN YOU CAN TOUCH ME... MAYBE.

BESIDES, IF YOU GOT TO HAVE JUGO...
THIS SWORD WILL DEFINITELY COME IN HANDY.

HEH.

OKAY, SASUKE. FROM HERE, LET'S SHOOT FOR WHICHEVER HIDEOUT IS CLOSER.
SHK

READ THIS WAY

UWAAHH!!
WHAM

OROCHIMARU MAY BE DEAD, BUT THAT DOESN'T LEAVE YOU FREE TO ACT AS YOU PLEASE!

!

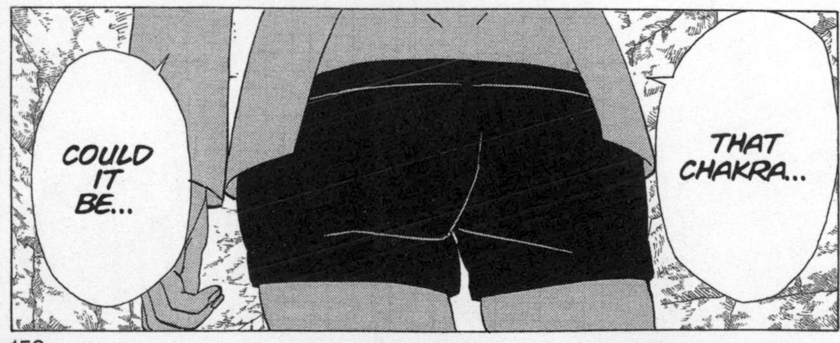
THAT CHAKRA...
COULD IT BE...

NARUTO

Number 348: And One Makes Three!!

SHOOSH

I HAVE TO ASK.
YEAH?

WHY ARE YOU DRAGGING A TEAM TOGETHER?

I HAVE A GOAL.
AND A SMALL TEAM...
...WILL LET ME REACH THAT GOAL FASTER.

OKAY... SO WHY ME?
EVER SINCE I JOINED OROCHI-MARU...
I'VE BEEN PREPARING FOR THIS. I ALWAYS TAKE NOTE OF SHINOBI WHO CATCH MY EYE.

READ THIS WAY

HEH ...

WELL, IF THAT'S YOUR GAME, YOU COULD DO BETTER THAN KARIN.
UNLIKE ME, SHE'S A TRUE BELIEVER.

SHE USED ME FOR EXPERI-MENTS.
SHE IRRITATES ME.

...

SURE. THERE ARE PLENTY OF OTHER SHINOBI JUST AS STRONG YET FAR EASIER TO HANDLE.
BUT SHE HAS A SPECIAL ABILITY ...
ONE THAT NO ONE ELSE POS-SESSES.

SH SHOOSH
TRUE... I CAN'T DENY THAT.

!

SHK
SHK

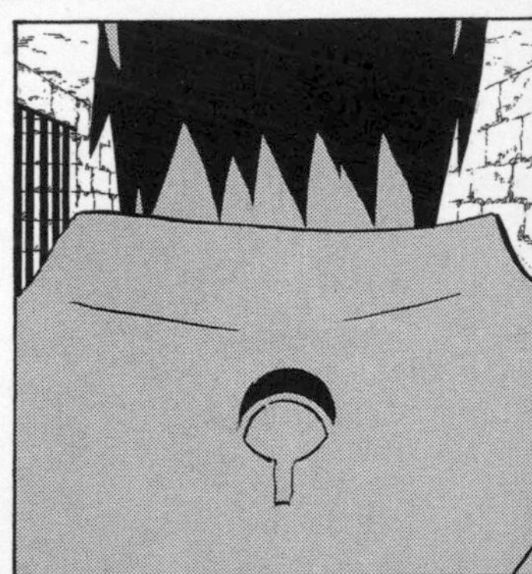

READ THIS WAY

ISN'T THAT... UCHIHA SASUKE?

WHY IS HE HERE?
WAIT... SASUKE... HERE ALONE ...WITHOUT OROCHI-MARU?
MAYBE IT WASN'T JUST A RUMOR?

IT MUST BE TRUE!
HE KILLED OROCHI-MARU!
AND HE'S COME TO SET US FREE!!

LISTEN TO YOUR-SELF. DON'T BE AN IDIOT.
OROCHI-MARU CAN'T BE DEFEATED.

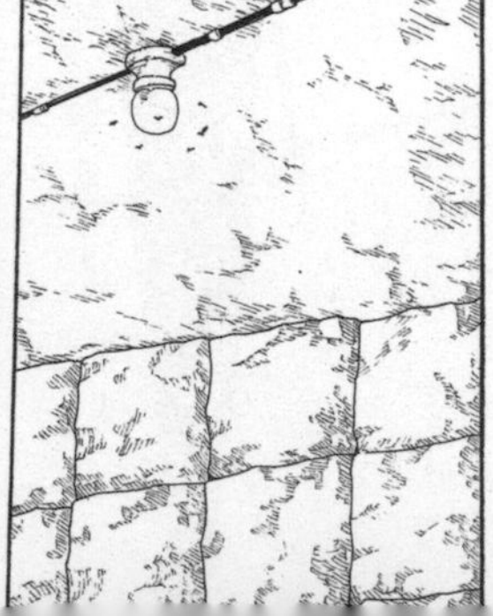

!
!

I KNEW IT WAS YOU TWO...

READ THIS WAY

SASUKE. WITHOUT A CHAPERONE, I SEE.
SO IT WASN'T JUST A RUMOR, WAS IT.

HEY, WHAT AM I, A HUNK OF MEAT?
ALL RIGHT... WHAT DO YOU WANT?

SASUKE WANTS TO TALK TO YOU.
SHOW US TO A ROOM WHERE WE CAN SIT DOWN AND CHAT I'M BUSHED. NOT USED TO WALKING SO FAR.

HMPH ...

KARIN, JOIN ME.
I NEED YOU.

YOU WHAH ?!
WHY ON EARTH SHOULD I? LISTEN, I'M IN CHARGE HERE!

OROCHIMARU IS GONE.
I'VE GOT RESPONSIBILITIES! WHAT ABOUT THE PRISONERS?!

SUIGETSU, GO AND LIBERATE EVERY PRISONER IN THE COMPOUND.

WHA...

HAA...
YOU AND THAT COMMANDING TONE OF VOICE...

READ
THIS
WAY

SST
DON'T YOU DARE!

THERE'S NO MORE NEED FOR A WARDEN. YOU DON'T HAVE TO STICK AROUND.
WHAT DO YOU SAY?

G-CHAK

I SAY NO THANKS!
I HAVE NO REASON TO JOIN YOU!!

...

FINE.
IF YOU'RE NOT INTERESTED, I'LL GO FIND SOMEONE ELSE.

UCHIHA SASUKE DID KILL OROCHIMARU!
YOU GOT IT.

SO...

THEN WHAT HAPPENS TO US?

YOU GO FREE, OF COURSE.

WHAT, YOU MEAN IT?

SURE. YOU DON'T SEE ME LOCKED UP, DO YOU?

READ THIS WAY

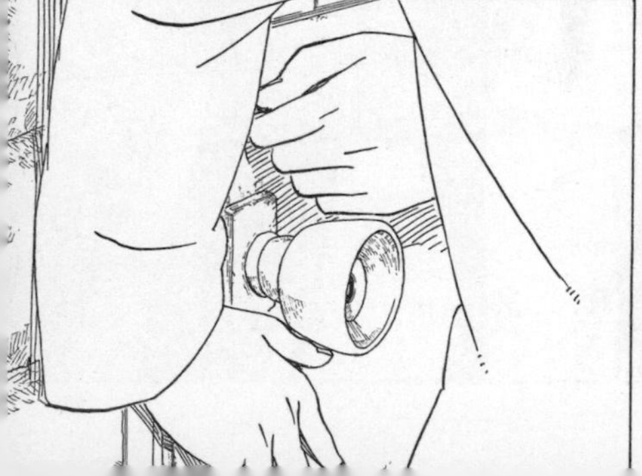

?

Okay, I'll come. ♡
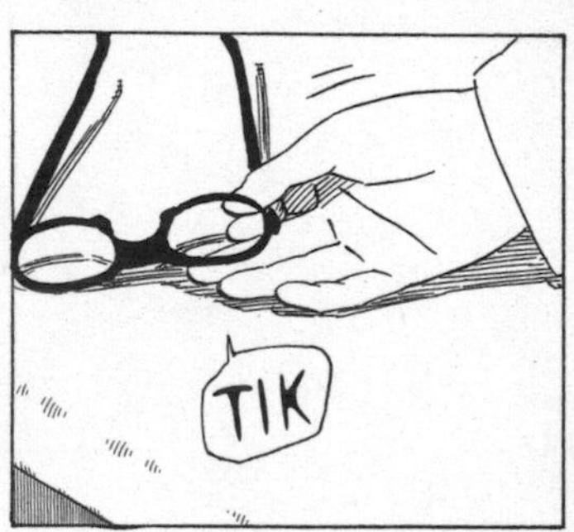
TIK

SST

IF YOU REALLY WANT ME TO, SASUKE...
I WILL FOLLOW YOU.
SST

READ THIS WAY

WHAT ARE YOU DOING?
ARE YOU ALWAYS THIS IMPUL-SIVE?

NO, I'VE PUT A LOT OF THOUGHT INTO THIS.
YOU'RE RIGHT. I'M FED UP WITH GUARDING THIS PLACE ANYWAY.

UH-OH ...THAT HELLCAT HAS LOCKED ME OUT...

HMPH...

HEY... GET BACK.
CREEP
Listen... Why don't we do this alone? Just the two of us?♡
Suigetsu won't do anything for you... not really.

SHRAK

C'MON, SASUKE. LET'S GO.
I TAKE IT KARIN IS STAYING HERE?

OH YEAH? WELL, THAT WORKS OUT OKAY.
WE CAN GO HALFWAY, THEN.

?

NOW... FOR JUGO.
SSS

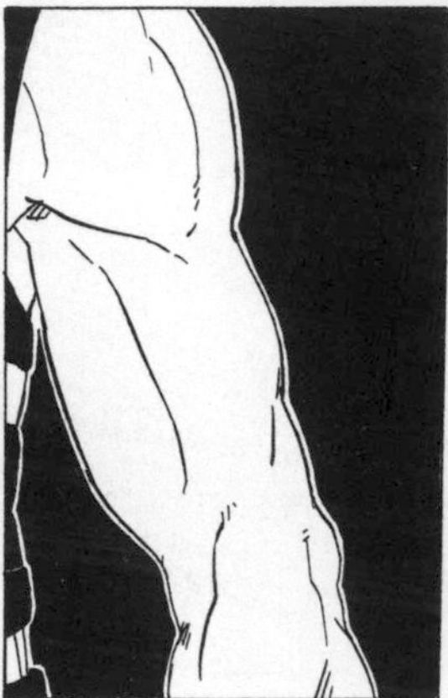

SURE. FINE. HALF-WAY.
SHOVE

DOES IT MATTER? IT'S NOT LIKE YOU'RE JOINING US ANYWAY.
WELL... WAIT, YOU WANNA PIECE OF ME?!
C'MON, THEN!

WHAAAT? JUGO?!
YOU'RE NOT THROW-ING HIM IN?

READ THIS WAY

...

NO... A WOMAN.
I PREFER A WOMAN.

BUT WAIT... WHY NOT A MAN?
YEAH... YEAH, A MAN WILL DO.

NO... A WOMAN... GOTTA BE A WOMAN...
NAH... A MAN'S BETTER...

NARUTO

Number 349: The Northern Hideout

...HUMAN EXPERIMENTATION.

IT'S FULL OF ALL THE MONSTERS THEY PRODUCE THERE.

Number 349: The Northern Hideout

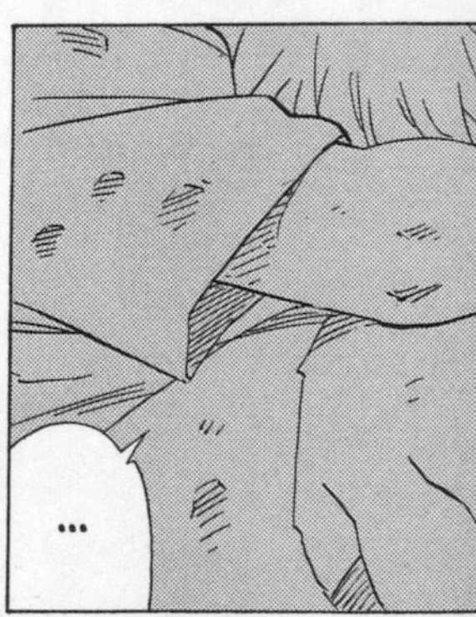

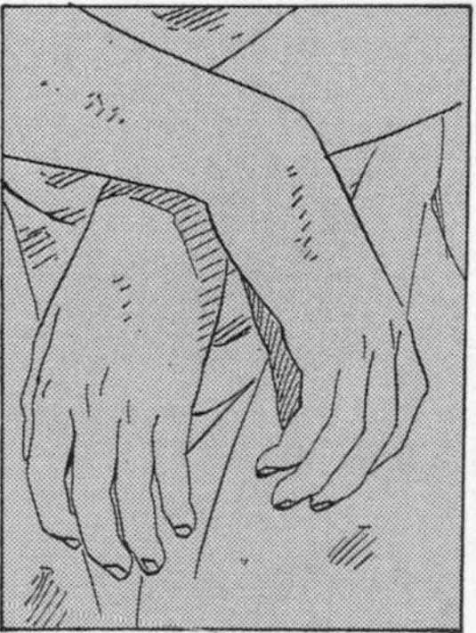

MY NEXT VICTIM...
...WILL BE A MAN... YEAH...

WHAM
GAHHHH!!
!

HMM... IT'S BEGUN...

HEY... YOU GOTTA BE TIRED BY NOW.
TIME FOR A BREAK.
SLURP

HOW PATHETIC *ARE* YOU?!
THE NORTHERN HIDEOUT IS STILL A LONG WAY OFF!

AND YOU'VE GOT SOME-WHERE ELSE TO GO.
DON'T WORRY ABOUT ME.
JUST GO ON AHEAD.

WELL, I JUST REMEMBERED SOMETHING I HAD TO DO AT THE NORTHERN HIDEOUT!
SO I DECIDED TO GO THERE FIRST!

OH BOY...

READ THIS WAY

...
SUIGETSU ...WHY ARE YOU HANGING AROUND WITH SASUKE?

I'VE GOT MY OWN REASONS.
YOU COULD SAY IT'S A MUTUALLY ADVAN-TAGEOUS RELATION-SHIP.

BUT HEY, I SHOULD ASK YOU THE SAME QUESTION.

I DON'T KNOW WHAT YOU GUYS ARE AFTER.
BUT YOU KNOW WHAT JUGO'S LIKE. DO YOU REALLY HOPE TO RECRUIT HIM?

I KNOW A FEW THINGS ABOUT HIM.
I WAS FORCED TO FIGHT HIM ONCE.

HE USED SOME INTERESTING POWERS AND WAS PRETTY STRONG.
BUT I COULD NEVER TELL WHAT HE WAS THINKING, AND I NEVER LIKED HIM.

RUMOR HAS IT HE CAME TO OROCHIMAKU OF HIS OWN WILL...
HE'S A LITTLE BIT DEMENTED.

...

DO YOU KNOW WHY HE CAME TO OROCHI-MARU?
BEATS ME. DIDN'T STRIKE ME AS ALL THAT BRIGHT.

...

...?

SO WHY DID HE?

TO BE FIXED.

FIXED?

YEAH.
THE HIDEOUT IS LIKE A SANCTUARY FOR HIM.

WHAT'S HIS PROB-LEM?

IT'S... LIKE AN ADDICTION. A COM-PULSION.
HE CAN'T DO ANYTHING ABOUT IT ON HIS OWN.

?

HE WANTS TO CONTROL HIS URGE TO SLAUGHTER.

READ
THIS
WAY

HE CAN USUALLY SUPPRESS HIS BIZARRE URGES.
BUT WHEN THEY OVER-COME HIM, HE'S NO LONGER HIMSELF.
HE TURNS INTO A HORRIBLE, DEMONIC THING. HIS LOOKS CHANGE ALONG WITH HIS PERSON-ALITY.

HUH. THE THINGS SOME PEOPLE HIDE.
WHEN I FOUGHT HIM THOUGH, HE USED A DIFFERENT KIND OF POWER...

OROCHIMARU WAS FASCI-NATED WITH HIS POWER. THAT'S WHAT LED HIM TO EXTRACT A CERTAIN FLUID FROM JUGO'S BODY...
AND PURIFY THE ENZYME...
WHICH ALLOWED OTHER SHINOBI TO ACHIEVE THE SAME STATE.

I'M SURE YOU KNOW WHERE I'M GOING HERE.

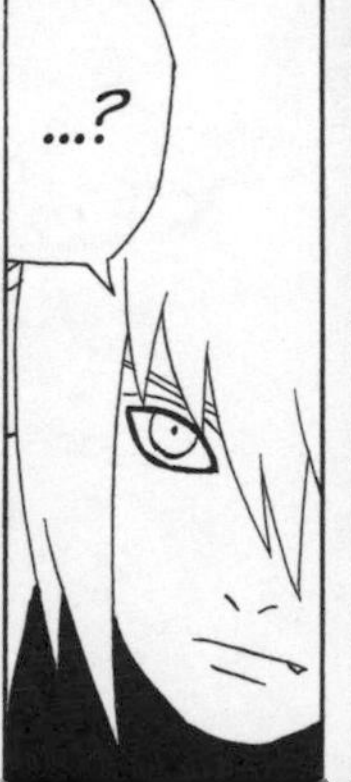
...?

I'M TALK-ING ABOUT ...

...THE CURSE MARK!

IT ORIGI- NATED WITH JUGO.
ZW
I'M GETTING OUT OF HERE. AND WHOEVER STANDS IN MY WAY... IS DEAD!
SO LET'S SEE... WHO'S NEXT?!
URR
RRRR

HEY... HOW ABOUT WE TAKE A BREAK?
THOMP
SUIGETSU! WE CAN'T KEEP STOPPING ALL THE TIME! COME ON, WE'RE ALMOST THERE!

IS IT THAT SWORD? IS IT TOO HEAVY FOR YOU?!
WHY DON'T YOU JUST LEAVE IT BEHIND?!
HEY...

?!

READ THIS WAY

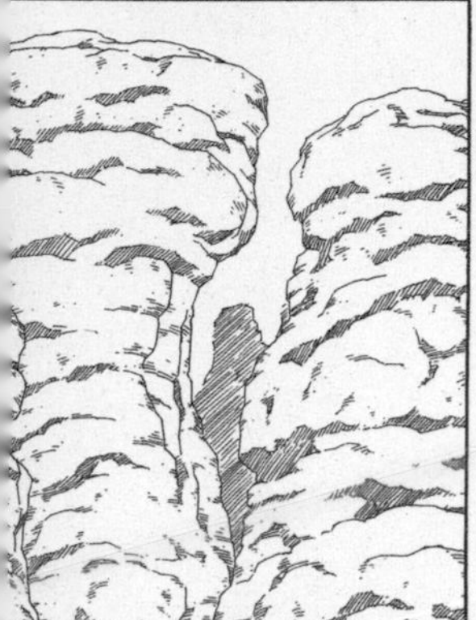

SLUMP

AGH...

THE WAY IT'S GOING ...

!

WHOOPS ...GUESS HE'S DEAD...

FWOO

KO
OM
I KNOW YOU...
WHAT IS THAT THING?
HE'S IN HIS SECOND STATE, BUT ALREADY TRANS-FORMED!
...

SHING

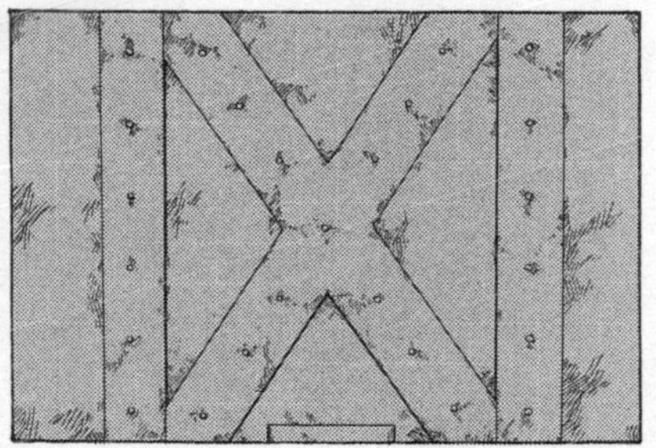

OKAY, IT'S SETTLED.
IF THE NEXT ONE THROUGH THAT DOOR IS A WOMAN, THEN I'LL KILL HER.
ZWURR

TO BE CONTINUED IN *NARUTO* VOLUME 39!

IN THE NEXT VOLUME...

uthor, planning,
d character design
ashi Kishimoto
ROAD TO NINJA
ロード・トゥ・ニンジャ
NARUTO THE MOVIE
For my friends and family, I'll risk my life for this mission!
ACTIONS FROM THE PAST RIPPLE INTO THE CURRENT AS NARUTO AND SAKURA ARE THRUST INTO A FAMILIAR, BUT VERY DIFFERENT VILLAGE HIDDEN IN THE LEAVES.
Available now on Blu-ray & DVD
Look for it in stores nationwide
© 2002 MASASHI KISHIMOTO /2007 SHIPPUDEN © NMP 2012
viz.com/naruto
viz media
SHONEN JUMP

You're Reading in the Wrong Direction!!

Whoops! Guess what? You're starting at the wrong end of the comic!

...It's true! In keeping with the original Japanese format, **Naruto** is meant to be read from right to left, starting in the upper-right corner.

Unlike English, which is read from left to right, Japanese is read from right to left, meaning that action, sound effects and word-balloon order are completely reversed... something which can make readers unfamiliar with Japanese feel pretty backwards themselves. For this reason, manga or Japanese comics published in the U.S. in English have sometimes been published "flopped"—that is, printed in exact reverse order, as though seen from the other side of a mirror.

By flopping pages, U.S. publishers can avoid confusing readers, but the compromise is not without its downside. For one thing, a character in a flopped manga series who once wore in the original Japanese version a T-shirt emblazoned with "M A Y" (as in "the merry month of") now wears one which reads "Y A M"! Additionally, many manga creators in Japan are themselves unhappy with the process, as some feel the mirror-imaging of their art alters their original intentions.

We are proud to bring you Masashi Kishimoto's **Naruto** in the original unflopped format. For now, though, turn to the other side of the book and let the ninjutsu begin...!

—Editor